The Yachtsman's
WEATHER GUIDE

The Yachtsman's
WEATHER GUIDE

Ingrid Holford

Airlife
England.

Front cover:
Moderate, force 4 wind, small waves becoming longer, 11-15 knots. *Patrick Roach*

Printed in England by Livesey Ltd., Shrewsbury.

Airlife Publishing Ltd.

7 St. John's Hill, Shrewsbury, England.

Contents

Introduction and Acknowledgements

This book is written for everyone who goes afloat and is at the mercy of the weather. I have stretched the word yacht to include everything from small dinghies to large cruisers, both sailing vessels and powered craft. I have also used the term yachtsman to include yachtswomen and yachtschildren, so that I may use *he* and *him* for everyone, to keep the text easy to read.

In this revised edition, I have taken heed of constructive comments made by reviewers 6 years ago, and tried to simplify some of the difficult topics, highlighted for me by sailing instructors and yachtsmen to whom I have lectured.

Meteorology is an imprecise science and forecasts are sometimes wrong, but rarely from negligence. The atmosphere is so vast that it cannot be monitored completely, even with satellites and remote self-recording instruments, and weather has an almost human ability to change its mind when a yachtsman is most vulnerable. That is when it is important to know how to make and use a weather chart from the Shipping Bulletin, in order to cope with deteriorating weather which may advance quicker than a yacht can travel.

Forget that much of meteorology is beyond the comprehension of most of us. Simply learn how to use the information provided by the professional, add your own local knowledge and logical reasoning based on the facts in this book, and the result will be forecasting at its best.

I should like to thank those who have contributed photographs to this book, acknowledged underneath all which are not my own. And my especial thanks go to Airlife Publishing Ltd who have been so successful in converting my ideas into the finished book.

1 Transmission of heat

Sunshine often seems a mere subsidiary bonus to yachtsmen compared with the wind, which determines the state of sea, drives a sailing boat and may be too strong an adversary even for powered yachts. However, the Sun is all-important because it is the heat source which determines all wind and weather.

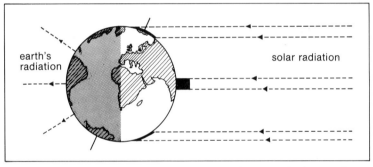

earth's radiation

solar radiation

Each hemisphere experiences seasons according to whether it tilts towards or away from the Sun, which is so far away that its rays are as good as parallel when they reach Earth. They provide more heat when concentrated over a small area from overhead than when they strike the Earth obliquely.

The Sun radiates electromagnetic waves, rather less than half of which penetrate our atmosphere and reach Earth's surface. There, the rays are reflected or absorbed in proportions which vary with the type of surface. Rough surfaces absorb more radiant energy than smooth surfaces, which are good reflectors; dark colours indicate better absorption qualities than light colours. The energy which is absorbed becomes heat and raises the temperature of the surface according to the material of which it is made. For instance, the temperature of a rock surface rises more with a given dose of sunshine than the same area of foliage.

Sunshine varies all the time. There may be obscuring cloud or obstructing mountains; the Sun may be high or low in the sky according to latitude or season; the Sun vanishes when the

Earth's rotation turns a place away from the Sun. Nor does the matter end there, because heat is a restless commodity, perpetually on the move from a hot to a colder surface by re-radiation, conduction or convection. The result is an extremely complicated pattern of temperatures over the Earth's surface, and these are significant in the weather context because of their effect upon the temperature of air.

Re-radiation of heat occurs from all surfaces on Earth, always from hotter to colder substances in the eternal busy attempt to balance the ration fairly. Materials which are good absorbers of heat are also good re-radiators, so that a person sunbathing on a dry beach benefits from two heat sources — direct from the Sun

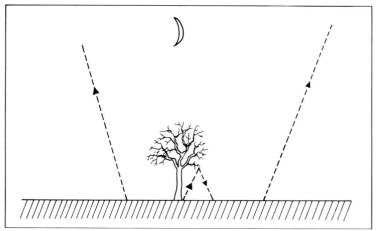

Cloudless skies permit the loss of heat away from Earth into the higher atmosphere.

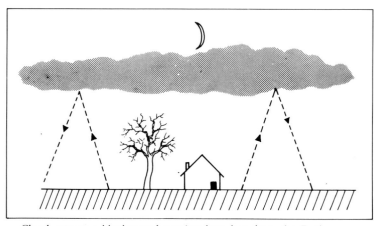

Cloud acts as a blanket and restricts heat loss from the Earth.

and also from the beach. However, during the day re-radiation is puny in the weather context compared with radiation from the Sun and it is only after dark that Earth's radiation becomes all important in determining weather. The ground and everything on it radiates heat which escapes into space unless there is some intervening blanket to absorb or reflect it back again towards the ground.

Cloud is an admirable insulator against heat loss at night and deters temperatures from falling far, but even the bare branches of a tree give some protection to whatever is below by intercepting re-radiated heat.

Conduction is the movement of heat from a warm to a colder area, within any one substance, or between two substances in direct contact with each other. Water is a good conductor, which makes it an excellent medium for cooking because it permits heat to spread evenly throughout the contents of the saucepan. It also permits heat from the Sun to spread throughout a considerable depth of sea water so that the temperature of the sea surface hardly changes from one day to another and only gradually builds up to a maximum by the end of summer. Shallows, of course, warm quickly on a sunny day because the volume of water involved is small.

Man overboard — body heat is quickly conducted away by water.

The rapidity with which water can conduct heat away from the human body makes it dangerous to capsize into cold water if one is unsuitably dressed. Since capsizing is a natural hazard in some sports like water skiing or dinghy sailing, the conductive properties of water have been used to good advantage in the design of wet suits. These are made of neoprene, a pliable synthetic material which is impervious to wind and water, and which must fit tightly to the body to deter infiltration under the edges if one is tipped into the sea. Any thin film of water which does seep in quickly warms to body temperature so that one is really clothed in a bath of hot water; many people put the suit on already wet, others find they soon enough get wet with perspiration during the rigours of their sport!

Air is a very poor conductor of heat, which makes it extremely useful in clothing to prevent loss of body heat during cold weather. The most efficient insulation consists of a honeycomb of air pockets and the best way to keep warm at sea (when not liable to capsize) is by wearing several layers of clothes, all with air between and each layer having a cellular structure, as in knitted fabrics. Always wear on the outside an impervious windcheater so that the wind cannot snatch away body heat which has seeped through the inside woollies.

Soil consists of millions of particles of rock, which heat quickly when exposed to direct radiation from the Sun. If the soil is dry, then the tiny air pockets which separate the particles insulate heat from seeping down into the soil, and most of the heat is used to boost the temperature of the surface. When the soil is wet, the water assists heat to spread over a greater depth of soil so that the temperature at the surface rises only a little. Vegetation, being mainly composed of water, warms very evenly in the sunshine and you are never likely to burn you hand by touching the surface of a leaf, though you may quite likely burn the soles of your feet over hot dry sand.

Air cools by conduction, and becomes more dense, when it rests above a surface colder than itself. When this surface is horizontal, the denser air remains in position to suffer still more cooling, only very slowly communicating heat loss to the layers of air above. On a still, cloudless night, air temperature at tree top level, for instance, is nearly always higher than air temperature near the ground. This is called an *inversion* because it is a reversal of the general rule that air temperatures are warmer near the ground than they are higher up in the atmosphere, beyond the influence of the warm surfaces on earth.

Wet soil is sometimes an ameliorating influence on a cloudless night when radiation of heat is liable to cause surface temperatures to fall. The soil itself may contain a useful store of heat, particularly after a good summer, and wet soil conducts it more easily to the surface than does dry soil. There, it counteracts radiated heat loss, so that the temperature of a wet soil surface falls less than that of a dry soil. However, if wet soil is covered in grass and weeds, then the insulating air pockets between the blades keeps the heat trapped in the soil beneath the grass surface.

Convection is a method of distributing heat within fluids. Air absorbs very little heat directly by electromagnetic radiation, and it is also a poor conductor of heat. In view of the fact that we live engulfed in air you may wonder how our environment ever gets warm at all. Air, however, has the advantage of being fluid and being able to move about according to rules of buoyancy. Each tiny volume of air which rests on a warming surface becomes hotter itself, less dense and rises upwards to make room for another colder and heavier parcel of air to warm in turn. Little by little air warms and moves on, until it engulfs the immediate environment, be that as small as a yacht's cabin or as large as the outdoors in which one is sailing.

Water distributes heat by upside-down convection, below the radiating surface rather than above as with convection in air. During the night the top thin layer of the sea cools by radiation, as does every other surface. As soon as it cools, however, it becomes more dense and sinks, allowing warmer water from below to well upwards to take its turn as the cooling surface. This continuous movement means that there are always slight differences of temperature between one patch of sea surface and another, but that the average surface temperature of the sea

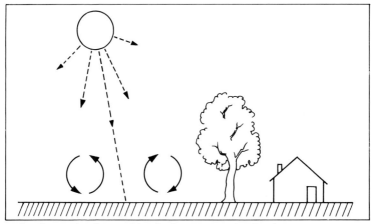

Land warming in sunshine leads to convection in air.

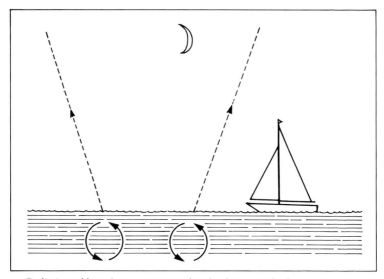

Radiation of heat from a water surface leads to upside-down convection within the water.

hardly alters in any one night. The surface temperature falls gradually to a minimum by the end of winter. Shallows cool much more rapidly than does deep water because the upwelling movements bring to the surface water which has previously cooled there. The surface temperature of rivers and estuaries, therefore, fluctuates more than deep sea does but less than the land does.

There is a peculiar difference, however, between fresh and salt water at low temperatures. Salt water gets progressively denser as it cools towards -1.5°C at which temperature it may start to freeze, depending upon how saline it is. Fresh water, however, is most dense at 4°C and thereafter becomes less dense as it cools further towards 0°C when it starts to freeze. Therefore, deep seas do not freeze because convection continually carries cold water downwards and replaces it with warmer water from below. Sea ice does form over shallows, where there is a limit to the amount of warmer replacement water below. Rivers ice over comparatively quickly if they cool steadily below 4°C because the coldest water then remains at the surface.

The perpetual liquidity of deep sea creates a potential hazard for those hardy people who continue yachting all through the winter. It is possible to be afloat when the air and the superstructure of a vessel has a temperature below 0°C. Wind may blow spray on to mast, cabin top, lifeboats, radar reflectors etc. where it will freeze. Ice can build up at an alarming rate and materially affect the stability of the yacht. Several trawlers, which carry a lot of equipment above decks, have been known to become top heavy with ice, capsized and sunk without trace. It is for this reason that, during the winter months, the British Shipping Bulletins always carry a statement of icing conditions in the SE Iceland sea area.

Weather results from the interaction of airs which have different temperature. Air temperature over the sea remains equable day and night, but over land it may fluctuate widely over short periods, sometimes being higher than over the sea, sometimes lower.

Food for thought

How do land temperatures fluctuate compared with sea temperatures?

Why is it dangerous to be capsized into the sea for even a short while?

At what temperature does shallow sea water usually start to freeze?

What is upside-down convection?

What is the danger of sailing in sub-freezing air temperatures?

2 Local winds

Wind is moving air and since it is invisible it is necessary to understand why, and therefore where, it forms. In our vast atmosphere there are winds within winds but since they all stem from the same basic cause, temperature difference, it may be helpful to visualize them first by domestic comparison.

Convection of air within a lit oven is a simple wind in an enclosed environment. Air warms on the heated sides, rises towards the top of the oven and cooler air from the centre takes its turn on the heating surfaces. This continuous movement eventually fills the oven with hot air, though the hottest always rises to the top. If you open the door, hot air escapes upwards into your face.

Conversely, by opening the door of a side-hinged refrigerator, dense cold air pours downwards on to your feet and the air flow is fastest when the temperature difference between kitchen and refrigerator is greatest. A top-opening freezer, however, can be opened without loss of cold air which settles snugly within four upright walls.

Oven and refrigerator, however, are only two self-contained units within many separate rooms which make up a whole house and there are likely to be differences in air temperature between them all, resulting in small winds. Air warming on a radiator surface gradually fills that room with hot air by convection. Air from an adjacent room without a radiator forces a passage under the door into the warmer room to give a howling draught. A cool hall may be warmer than the outside air which pushes in through a window frame, producing still more draught. These familiar little winds within the home are similar to small scale winds outdoors.

Zephyrs blow near the banks of rivers or small lakes even when there is not enough wind further away to stir the flag on a flag staff. Tiny movements of air arise because a stony towpath warms more than an adjoining field, and both warm more than the river itself. You can't see these zephyrs, they hardly rustle the bushes; cynics may say there is no wind at all. Yet the alert dinghy sailor knows they exist and catches enough in the sail to make progress when none seemed possible.

Tiny zephyrs keep dinghies moving on the river in apparently calm weather.

An anabatic wind blows upslope during the early morning when the sun is shining and there are no other winds to confuse the issue. A hill or mountain side facing the Sun gets a marginal start in the heat benefits because low angled rays concentrate on to a smaller area of the slope than they do over flat ground. The air nearest to the slope warms, rises upwards and is replaced by

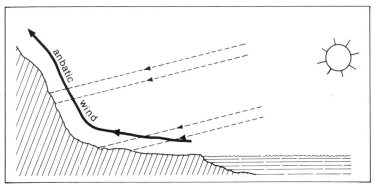

The anabatic wind blows upslope early on sunny mornings

cooler air over the valley. If the mountain adjoins lake or sea the early air flow towards the slope may be very useful for a sailing boat, but the anabatic wind is usually only discernible as a separate entity until the sun has risen high enough to stir up the air over the whole land surface. The on-shore wind may persist and intensify but will not necessarily pull towards the hill side. **The sea breeze** develops in coastal areas whenever the Sun is high enough to warm the land appreciably above the temperature of the sea. All the year around in the tropics but between April and September in temperate latitudes; mostly in bright sunshine but sometimes when the Sun shines weakly through thin cloud

Rising air over the land is replaced by colder air from over the sea and gradually develops into an off-sea wind, detectable several miles out at sea and perhaps 15-20 miles inland. The sea breeze sets in a little earlier each day as spring advances to summer, a little later as autumn approaches. Being dependent upon the Sun, however, it ceases every late afternoon, a fact to remember when planning a journey.

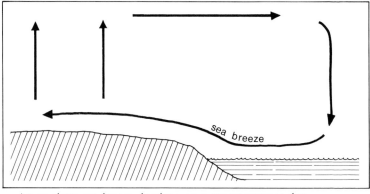

An on-shore sea breeze develops on a sunny summer day

When the sea breeze is the only appreciable wind, it blows directly on-shore to begin with, and mainly close to land. However, as it develops in horizontal and vertical extent during the day the forces exerted by the rotating Earth deflect it to the right (in the northern hemisphere) so that it blows more nearly parallel to the coast line. In complicated areas, like the Solent, where air rises over both the Isle of Wight and the mainland, the sea breeze may operate in both directions to begin with until the stronger mainland breeze takes over.

However, the sea breeze often has to come to terms with a larger scale pressure wind (Chapter 4). If that, too, is blowing on-shore, it will augment the sea breeze; if the pressure wind blows off-shore, it may at first counteract the sea breeze. Paradoxically, however, later in the day the off-shore upper winds may reinforce the downdraughts over the sea which feed the sea breeze and thereby make the sea level breeze on to shore more effective. Pressure winds which blow at an angle to the shore affect the direction of the sea breeze, but there are no hard and fast rules which apply to all areas. If about to sail in unfamiliar waters, enquire of a local yachtsman what the sea breeze habits are in that area.

A katabatic wind is a downslope wind which develops when cloudless skies result in radiation cooling of the land at night. The side of any hill or mountain cools and so does the air in contact with it. The dense air slides downhill and is replaced by warmer air from the same level above the valley, until an appreciable wind blows. The katabatic wind is strongest during long nights and down steep slopes, reaching gale force in such

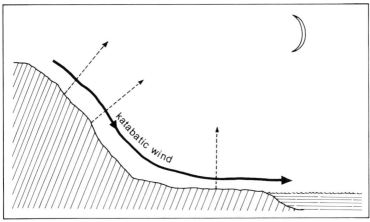

A katabatic wind blows down slope on cloudless nights when there is negligible pressure wind

extreme cases as the mountains of Antarctica and Greenland. Such environments, however, are not usual haunts for yachtsmen but quite useful katabatics can be gleamed from the steep sides of fiords or lochs in temperate climates, even on a summer night.

A land breeze may form at night when the land cools on cloudless nights until the air above it becomes colder than the air over the sea and flows off-shore. This does not usually happen till several hours after dark and the breeze is not usually important to a yachtsman unless the coast is hilly enough to permit gravity drainage of the cold air. In which case, the land breeze is better described as a katabatic wind.

We must now discuss the larger scale circulation of air throughout the Earth's atmosphere, because such winds, if strong, may nullify any of the local and shallow winds we have discussed in this chapter.

Food for Thought
What is wind?
How does the sea breeze form?
What happens to the sea breeze at night?
What wind blows near high ground on an otherwise calm, cloudless night?
What is an anabatic wind?
What happens to an on-shore sea breeze as the day progresses?
In what season of the year can one expect a sea breeze around the British Isles?

3 Atmospheric pressure

The troposphere is the name given to the whole lower atmosphere in which weather forms. Its characteristic is that air temperature, in general, decreases with increased altitude and inversions of temperature are temporary modifications. The tropopause is the height at which air temperature ceases to fall with increase of altitude and this boundary is higher above the equator than above the poles. Hence, even though the air at the equator is much warmer near the ground than it is at the poles, air cools progressively to an average height of 10 miles above the equator, at which height it may be colder than air at the same height above the poles, where the average height of the tropopause is nearer 6 miles. Any general tendency, therefore, for cold air to flow from the poles towards the equator at ground level is offset by a tendency for air many miles above the equator to flow polewards. The balance of the atmosphere is achieved in several huge vertical cellular movements, rather than in single movements between equator and poles. Air rises over the equator, sinks again around the 30° lines of latitude, rises again in the region around 60° latitudes and sinks again over the poles. This very broad principle is confused still more because of

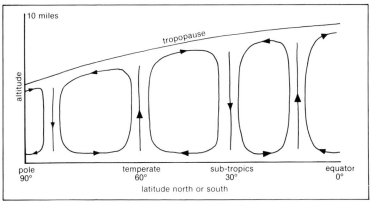

The balance of Earth's atmosphere is achieved by huge vertical cellular movements

the intervening patchwork of contrasting sea and land surfaces, all with different temperatures, so that the movements of air throughout the whole atmosphere might seem impossible to predict. Mercifully for both meteorologists and yachtsmen, Torricelli invented the barometer and Buys Ballot used it to formulate a rule of breathtaking simplicity by which to 'see' the major winds blowing around the world.

Atmospheric pressure was discovered by Torricelli in 1643 when he experimented with a tube full of mercury, whose open end he inverted into a cistern which also contained mercury. The level in the tube fell, but not so far as to equalize with the level in the cistern. Torricelli deduced, rightly, that the atmosphere had weight and was exerting a pressure which balanced the mercury inside the tube, above which there was a vacuum. Blaise Pascal confirmed the matter by arranging for a Torricelli tube to be

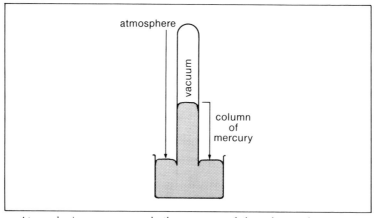

Atmospheric pressure equals the pressure of the column of mercury.

carried up a mountain, when the mercury was found to fall *en route.*. In other words, the higher one penetrates upwards into the atmosphere, the lower becomes the pressure. The length of the mercury column in the tube was found to vary every day and from one place to another, and although scientists were convinced that the changes were in some way connected with the weather, it took some time to discover how.

The aneroid barometer was invented in 1843 by Lucien Vidi and consists essentially of corrugated metal capsules partially evacuated of air, which expand or contract according to changes of the outside atmospheric pressure. This is a sturdy instrument, free from the breakage and spillage problems inherent in mercury barometers, and eminently suitable for domestic or yachting use. Admiral Fitzroy, who was Chief Meteorologist to the Board

Aneroid barometer; inch & millibar scale

of Trade in the 1850s, did his utmost to ensure that the aneroid barometer was standard equipment on all ships. From constant observation he was certain that movements in pressure advertised improvements or deterioration in the weather, and the years have proved him right. Any yacht large enough to cruise, as opposed to just racing around local buoys, should carry a barometer and every yachtsman should learn to understand its message. Tendency is more important than actual value of any one reading, so it is important to take regular readings and set the indicator arm every time. This is movable by a knob set on the face of the glass and it should be aligned so that it rests immediately over the needle which is recording pressure. Then, the discrepancy between the stationary indicator and the pressure needle when read on the next occasion indicates whether pressure has risen or fallen in the interval. The pressure value needle can be adjusted from the back of the barometer and should be used occasionally to align the barometer reading with a check value supplied by a local weather office or coastguard station. Absolute precision is not essential, so long as the barometer is undamaged and therefore fluctuating correctly.

A barograph is a self-recording barometer, whose pressure mechanism is linked by arm and inked nib to a drum which rotates by clockwork and carries a chart graduated for time and pressure. This is a fascinating instrument to have at home, if you can afford one, but it is not always suitable for a small yacht.

Battery barograph with drum mounting designed to accept severe motion in a small yacht at sea. Disposable twelve month inked pen nib *Bray Developments Co.*

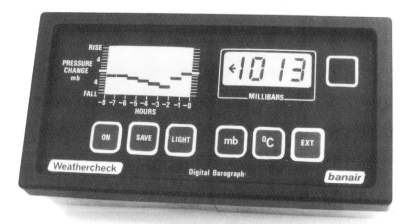

Digital barograph, giving pressure value at each hour and storing information for an eight hour period, for display on screen. Compensated for temperature, with eight hour storage facility for cabin air temperature. Sea water thermometer, for in-hull fixing, available as an extra; useful for those cruising the ocean currents where sea fog is a hazard. *Banair, Southampton.*

Just as practical, even though not retaining a permanent record of pressure, is the digital barograph illustrated. It records pressure at each hour and stores for a period of 8 hours, displaying on screen at the touch of a button in bold stepped intervals which are easy to read in a dim cabin. Immediate update of pressure for 5 second display if needed.

Mean sea level pressure is atmospheric pressure corrected for the altitude at which the reading is made. Pressure recorded on a mountain top is considerably lower than pressure recorded at the same time by a barometer immediately below at sea level. The difference, however, has nothing to do with any weather factor, it merely reflects the altitude of the instrument. In order to iron out such discrepancies of topography and make all pressure readings comparable for meteorological purposes, an imaginary column of air, equal to the height of the instrument above sea level, is added to the instrument reading. People living on high ground can adjust their instruments permanently so that they always read MSL pressure.

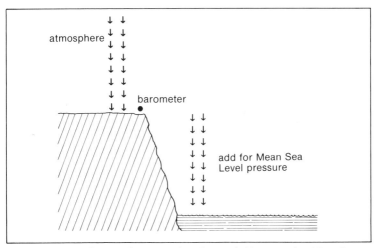

Pressure provides significant weather clues only if corrected to Mean Sea Level (MSL)

The millibar is the modern international unit for measuring atmospheric pressure. (Some organisations call the same unit a hectopascal, in memory of the scientist, Pascal.)

1 millibar (mb)	= 100 Newtons per square metre
1000 mb	= the pressure exerted by 29.53 inches or 750.06mm of mercury at 32°F (0°C)

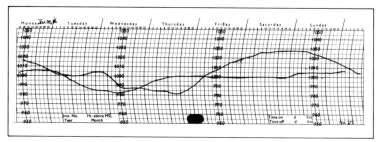

Typical 2 weeks' undulation of pressure in Great Britain

All meteorological offices transmit pressure information in millibars, hence it is important for yacht barometers to carry this scale, even though a second scale may record in inches or millimetres of mercury.

The possible range of atmospheric pressure is considerable. Some places, particularly remote islands in the low pressure belt 15-20° north and south of the equator, have remarkably constant pressure which varies little from the theoretical 'standard atmospheric pressure' of 1013.25 mb. In the British Isles, barograph charts are usually scaled from 960 mb to 1050 mb and it is the space between 980 mb and 1030 mb which gets most used, although values soar or fall towards either end of the range at times. However, pressure often climbs much higher than 1050 mb over the centre of large continents in winter (1083.8 mb has been recorded at Agata in north central Siberia) and pressure plumbs to unknown depths at the centre of the most vicious low pressure systems. 877 mb has been recorded by instruments dropped by the US Air Force into the eye of a typhoon and pressure probably falls even lower at the centre of tornadoes. Few instruments have ever been strategically placed to measure the central pressure.

Food for Thought
Why is there a movable pointer on the dial face of a barometer?
What correction must be made to a barometer reading before its pressure value is significant for determining weather?
In what approximate latitudes are the semipermanent high pressure belts?
What is the tropopause?
How many millibars are there in a hectopascal?

4 Synoptic charts and pressure winds

Synoptic weather observations are descriptions of the weather existing at different places at the same time, summarized into numerical code for easy transmission. Teleprinters, radio and electronic instruments pour out a constant stream of five or six figure messages which tell meteorologists more about existing

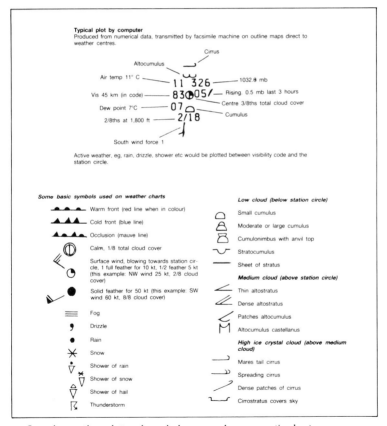

Typical plot by computer
Produced from numerical data, transmitted by facsimile machine on outline maps direct to weather centres.

Cirrus

Altocumulus

Air temp 11° C ———— 1032.8 mb

Vis 45 km (in code) ———— Rising. 0.5 mb last 3 hours

Dew point 7°C ———— Centre 3/8ths total cloud cover

2/8ths at 1,800 ft ———— Cumulus

South wind force 1

Active weather, eg, rain, drizzle, shower etc would be plotted between visibility code and the station circle.

Some basic symbols used on weather charts

Warm front (red line when in colour)

Cold front (blue line)

Occlusion (mauve line)

Calm, 1/8 total cloud cover

Surface wind, blowing towards station circle, 1 full feather for 10 kt, 1/2 feather 5 kt (this example: NW wind 25 kt, 2/8 cloud cover)

Solid feather for 50 kt (this example: SW wind 60 kt, 8/8 cloud cover)

Fog

Drizzle

Rain

Snow

Shower of rain

Shower of snow

Shower of hail

Thunderstorm

Low cloud (below station circle)

Small cumulus

Moderate or large cumulus

Cumulonimbus with anvil top

Stratocumulus

Sheet of stratus

Medium cloud (above station circle)

Thin altostratus

Dense altostratus

Patches altocumulus

Altocumulus castellanus

High ice crystal cloud (above medium cloud)

Mares tail cirrus

Spreading cirrus

Dense patches of cirrus

Cirrostratus covers sky

Sample weather plot and symbols, as used on synoptic charts.

weather than could any spoken message ten times as long. These observations are plotted on to maps, with internationally agreed code symbols or numerals, at the location they were made. Every weather factor has its set position around the station circle, providing an international pictorial language. Among the most important values on any synoptic chart is atmospheric pressure, both the actual value at the time of the observation and also the tendency (rise, fall or steady) over the past three hours. Pressure value is plotted outside the top right hand quadrant of the weather station circle with pictorial representation of tendency just below.

An isobar is a line on a map which joins places having equal atmospheric pressure at that time. A series of isobars, generally drawn for even values of pressure either side of 1000 mb, creates a pressure contour map analogous to a geographical contour map. Each isobar is a closed circuit around a centre of high or low pressure and no line crosses another — that would give two values at one place, which is impossible. Pressure usually changes smoothly from one place to another in the same locality, so that it is possible, within limits, to interpolate or extrapolate from a few known values to ascertain others.

The pressure gradient is the rate of pressure change across the isobars and is analogous to the gradient of a hill. The closer

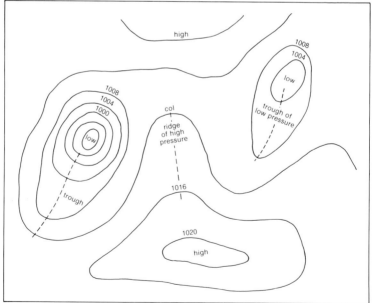

Typical fluid pattern of isobars, showing pressure gradient.

together the isobars, the steeper is the pressure gradient. Buys Ballot was the Dutchman, who, in 1857, formulated the connection between isobars and the major winds of the world.

Air tries to flow from a region of high pressure to one of low pressure but only achieves this near the equator. Elsewhere air is deflected from the straightforward high-to-low direction by the geostrophic force caused by the Earth's rotation on its axis. At altitudes above 2000 ft, assumed to be beyond the influence of surface friction, wind is deflected 90° from the high-to- low direction and blows parallel with the isobars. At surface level, friction keeps a tighter hold upon moving air which blows more nearly to its instinctive high-to-low direction; approximately 30° to the isobars over rough ground and about 10° to the isobars even over the sea.

There are of course two directions which can be described as parallel to the isobars, in just the same way as there are two directions in which one can drive a car parallel to the kerb of a road. The geostrophic wind obeys rules which are just as explicit as those which govern motor traffic flow, and these rules are given in Buys Ballot's Law.

The rule is different for the northern and southern hemispheres, because each is upside-down to the other although both rotate in the same direction about a common axis. If isobars are to be a helpful tool, it is essential that yachtsmen can read a synoptic chart quickly and correctly. It is suggested, therefore, that you read and memorize *only* the rule for the particular hemisphere which concerns you. There will be time enough to learn the other when you visit the opposite side of the world. Remember, however, that whichever hemisphere you are in, and despite the differing wind rules, there is convergence of air towards centres of low pressure and divergence from centres of high. This is important in the processes which create cloud and rain.

Wind speed at 2000 ft above the ground can be read from an isobaric chart, by using a scale calibrated for the map being used. Most blank maps which are printed for use as synoptic charts carry a geostrophic scale for the purpose. Place the scale at right angles to the isobars in the region of the map for which a reading is required, the highest end of the scale on one isobar. The reading given by the scale at the point of intersection with the next isobar gives wind speed at 2000 ft. Make sure the scale is graduated for the same interval of pressure as the isobars drawn on the map. If the scale is graduated for 2 mb intervals and the isobars are drawn for 4 mb intervals, then double the wind speed indicated on the scale. If the isobars are drawn at 1 mb intervals, then read your 2 mb scale at its intersection with

Buys Ballot's Law — Northern Hemisphere

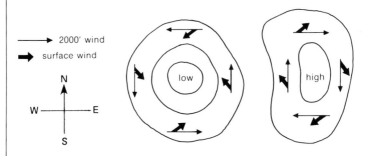

The wind at 2000 ft blows parallel to the isobars so that low pressure is on the left hand when the wind is on your back. This means *anticlockwise round low* pressure and *clockwise around high*.

Surface wind is always backed (ie in an anticlockwise sense) from the 2000 ft wind and therefore converges towards a centre of low pressure but diverges from a centre of high.

Buys Ballot's Law — Southern Hemisphere

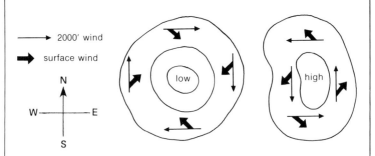

The wind at 2000 ft blows parallel to the isobars so that low pressure is on the right hand when the wind is on your back. This means *clockwise round low* pressure and *anticlockwise around high*.

Surface wind is always veered (ie in a clockwise sense) from the 2000 ft wind and therefore converges towards a centre of low pressure but diverges from a centre of high.

the next-but-one isobar. Providing that you always use the same scale map practice soon enables you to size up the wind at a glance. Tightly packed isobars crowding the chart warn you back to harbour; a few widely spaced isobars indicate that the pressure wind alone may be uselessly light for sailing and all hope must be placed on the possibility of a sea breeze.

Wind speed close to the river or sea is, of course, what interests yachtsmen. The surface wind is slower than that at 2000 ft because of the drag of surface friction, being on average ⅓ the speed of the pressure wind over rough land and about ⅔ the speed over calm sea. However, average surface wind is rather an unrealistic concept because turbulence creates frequent fluctuations in the lower levels of air. Wind may gust to a speed equal to that at 2000 ft one minute and then lull to almost nothing the next, even during gales. Moreover, wind direction alters at the same time, because gusts of stronger air brought down from higher levels momentarily retain the direction in which they were blowing there. Consequently, surface wind is never steady and the wisest policy is to budget for the wind strength and direction as indicated by the isobars when considering the extremes of wind likely to be encountered.

Wind behaves very much like water when encountering obstructions. Air cannot stop, so it changes direction to divert around the sides or over the top of any obstacle in its path, and on the leeward side eddies backwards rather like water whirlpools. Therefore, guard against judging wind direction by a burgee in the lee of a sailshed and watch for deviations in wind direction when rounding prominent headlands. Anticipate back eddies behind river walls and use them to advantage when racing in fitful wind.

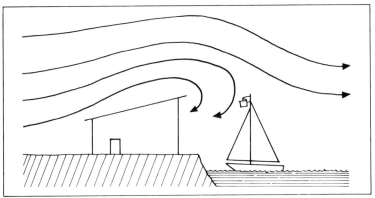

Nearby obstacles may cause a burgee to give false information about wind direction

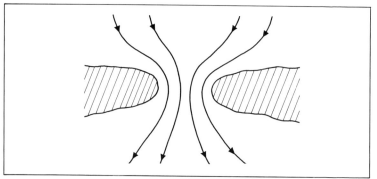

Wind alters in direction and increases in speed when funnelled through a valley (plan view)

Wind speed increases when moving around or over the top of obstructions because air has to move through a smaller space than the same volume of air elsewhere. So beware of vicious wind slams around a harbour wall or headland if the wind is

Tree and hedge, shaped by persistent battering by the wind, typical of coasts fully exposed to prevailing wind

Flowering broom shreds to nothing the light wind blowing across the wall

from an appropriate direction. Wind which funnels through a constriction, such as a row of houses or between two hills is liable to burst out at the end like tap water forced through the nozzle of a garden hose. Quite minor constrictions can result in excesses of wind capable of capsizing an unwary helmsman, and even the largest yachts seek shelter or sea room from the Mistral, a northerly wind funnelling down the Rhone Valley which quickly turns the Gulf of Lyons into a seething cauldron.

Semi-permeable barriers, such as trees, bushes and hedges permit the passage of air, but shred the wind into confused movements, which considerably reduces its impact. Such barriers give admirable protection for gardens and fields but are not favourite landscape features for yachtsmen who actually *want* wind to drive their boats. It has been calculated that a close vegetation barrier diminishes wind speed for a total distance downwind of about 20 times the height of the barrier, with wind speed reduced to a minimum of 20% within a distance of 5 times the height of the barrier. But meteorology does not really lend itself to such precise arithmetic, and if these figures were universally true river sailors would never progress at all behind the copses lining the banks. Somehow wind pushes through to give sailing wind beyond and often the most trying features are not trees, with relatively uncluttered trunks, but scrub and saplings sprawling low to the ground. The sad fact is that the general public and yachtsmen look at their environment with different eyes. Consider the picture of the waterworks wall at Surbiton, on the Thames near London where years of patience have encouraged a 10 ft hedge of broom to grow along the top. It disguises the ugly brickwork to perfection, specially when in full bloom, but it shreds to nothing any light wind blowing from that side of the river, to the dinghy sailors' despair.

Moderate breeze force 4; small waves becoming longer, fairly frequent white horses.

The Beaufort Scale of Wind Force was introduced by Commander Francis Beaufort in 1805 and was an excellent attempt at measuring the strength of the wind at a time when there were no instruments to measure velocity. The Beaufort Scale grades wind strength according to the effect of invisible air on visible things, and the original Scale related to the amount of canvas sailing ships could carry. This was soon superseded by a less subjective criterion, the effect of local wind strength upon the sea, and the waves created. Landlubbers have now got their version of the Beaufort Scale too, and both versions are included here since it is as important to size up the wind before leaving the shore as it is to assess it when afloat.

Each Beaufort Force on the Scale has been translated into a range of wind speeds as measured by modern instruments. Beware of thinking that these Forces are the same as the

BEAUFORT WIND SCALE

Force	Description	Land specifications	Sea specifications	Equivalent speeds Knots	Miles per hour
0	Calm	Smoke rises vertically.	Sea like a mirror.	—	—
1	Light air	Direction of wind shown by smoke drift, but not by wind vanes.	Ripples with the appearance of scales are formed.	1-3	1-3
2	Light breeze	Wind felt on face; leaves rustle, ordinary vane moved by wind.	Small wavelets, still short but more pronounced.	4-6	4-7
3	Gentle breeze	Leaves and small twigs in constant motion; wind extends light flag.	Large wavelets. Crests begin to break.	7-10	8-12
4	Moderate	Raises dust and loose paper, small branches are moved.	Small waves becoming longer, fairly frequent white horses.	11-15	13-18
5	Fresh	Small trees in leaf begin to sway; crest wavelets form on inland waters.	Moderate waves taking a more pronounced long form, many white horses formed. Chance of spray.	16-21	19-24
6	Strong	Large branches in motion; whistling heard in telegraph wires; umbrellas used with difficulty.	Large waves beginning to form; the white foam crests are more extensive everywhere. Probably some spray.	22-27	25-31
7	Near gale	Whole trees in motion; inconvenience felt when walking against wind.	Sea heaps up and white foam from breaking waves begins to be blown in streaks along the direction of the wind.	28-33	32-38
8	Gale	Breaks twigs off trees; generally impedes progress.	Moderately high waves of greater length; edges of crests begin to break into the spindrift.	34-40	39-46
9	Severe gale	Slight structural damage occurs (chimney pots and slates are removed).	High waves. Dense streaks of foam along the direction of the wind. Crests of waves begin to topple, tumble and roll over. Spray may affect visibility.	41-47	47-54
10	Storm	Seldom experienced inland; trees uprooted; considerable structural damage occurs.	Very high waves with long overhanging crests. The resulting foam is blown in dense white streaks along the direction of the wind.	48-55	55-63
11	Violent storm	Widespread damage.	Exceptionally high waves, sometimes concealing small and medium ships. Sea completely covered with long white patches of foam. Edges of wave crests blown into froth. Poor visibility.	56-63	64-73
12	Hurricane	Widespread damage.	Air filled with foam and spray, sea white with driving spray. Visibility bad.	>64	>74

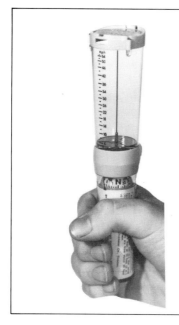

Ventimeter wind gauge.

The force of the wind into an opening causes a plastic float to rise in the instrument and record wind speed.

physical force which wind exerts upon your driving sails. In fact, the physical force is directly proportional to the square of the wind speed, thus making the impact of gusts particularly powerful

Swell is wave motion caused by wind which is blowing elsewhere, and may herald a storm long before the wind and cloud symptoms appear locally. There are huge swell waves called South Atlantic Rollers in southern latitudes where there are few land masses to interrupt the motion of the sea.

'The weight in the wind' is a nautical expression which does not usually appear in meteorological text books but which is a very appropriate description of certain conditions experienced by sailing craft. The term has little to do with density of air because although cold air is denser than warm air, the difference is negligible compared with the amount of air (i.e. wind) which presses on a sail.

The force exerted by wind is directly proportional to the square of the wind speed, so that if speed doubles in a gust then the force which it exerts increases fourfold. This means that a yacht becomes as difficult to handle as a bucking bronco in particularly gusty weather and gives the impression of 'weight'.

Gustiness is characteristic of convection situations, when air warming over any surface rises and is replaced by stronger gusts from higher up. Inland yachtsmen, whose sailing waters are

Wind sock blows down-wind from staff, indicating strength of wind by nearness to horizontal position. Arrow head on wind vane points to direction *from which* the wind is blowing, with broad fin always downwind. Rotating cups of anemometer register wind speed electrically on dial in cabin

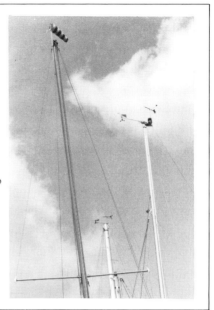

Weighty winds occur when cold air overrides warmer water, creating frequent gusts on the sails.

usually insignificant in area compared with the surrounding land, experience weighty wind whenever there is strong convection over the land in summer, which is fairly frequent. On the same day at sea, surface temperature remains constant, there may be no convection and fairly smooth wind conditions prevail. Weighty winds do occur at sea, however, whenever the sea is warmer than the wind blowing across it. Along the east coast of Great Britain, for instance, a cold easterly wind in winter from Europe travelling across the comparatively warm North Sea registers as weighty, whereas on the same day inland, where the land has quickly adapted to the temperature of the air stream, the wind is probably remarkably steady. American yachtsmen experience weighty wind, even in summer, when a cool northerly air stream blows across the warm Gulf Stream. Anywhere in the world, at any season, a weighty wind can be predicted if a cool airstream can be 'seen' from the isobars to be blowing across a surface, land or sea, which is known to be, or become, warmer than the air by at least 5 Celsius degrees.

Food for Thought
What are *synoptic* weather observations?
What is an isobar?
How does surface wind differ from that at 2000 ft?
What happens when wind is forced to surmount an obstacle?
What happens to wind when funnelled along constricting valleys?
What is swell?
How does the force exerted on a sail alter if wind speed doubles in a gust?
What wind speed is meant if described as strong, force 6?
How does wind blow around a centre of low pressure a) in the Northern hemisphere b) in the Southern?

5 Water vapour in the air

Weather is closely connected with wind direction and the disposition of land and sea. The patterns which isobars make on a synoptic chart can, with a little practice, tell you at a glance the type of weather which exists; and the way the patterns change with time provides the basis for weather forecasting. The processes by which weather forms are the same the world over, only the quantity of the ingredients varies.

Water vapour is always present in the air, even on a fine clear day. It is acquired mainly from the seas of the world, in large quantities if the wind has·travelled across them for a long distance. Air which has blown across a large expanse of land is comparatively dry. In Great Britain, for instance, southwesterly winds are nearly always moist on arrival, while easterly winds from Europe are dry. The small islands which dot the middle of the Pacific Ocean are nearly always enveloped in moist air, whichever way the wind blows.

However, air has a maximum capacity for water vapour at any particular temperature. The warmer the air the greater the capacity, even if it not actually full up (saturated). The colder the air the smaller its possible vapour content. Think of air as a hotel with a maximum capacity for guests, but which may only be part occupied at any one time. Obviously, the smaller the hotel the less the capacity for guests; and if the larger hotel, only part occupied, closes down some rooms for maintenance, the time may come when it is full up. Any further closure of rooms means some guests must be turned out. In weather terms, if air temperature falls to dew point, at which vapour content is the maximum possible, any further cooling must result in spillage of vapour as condensation.

The detective work of weather forecasting can be summarised as a search for clues about what is likely to cause air temperature to fall below, or rise above, dew point. This is not as simple as it sounds. because there are many and often contradictory factors determining air temperature and many possible variations in the amount of water vapour present.

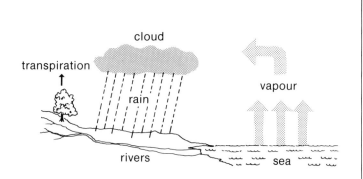

The water cycle processes one global supply over and over again, by evaporation from the seas, condensation as cloud and precipitation, transpiration of vapour from plants, and return of water in rivers to the seas again.

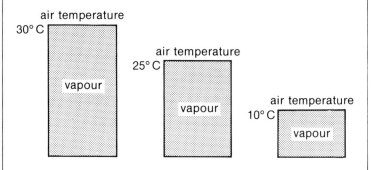

Warm air *can* hold more vapour than cold air.

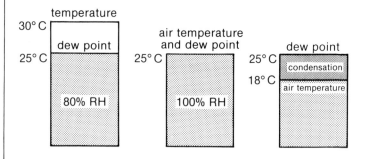

When clear air, less than saturated cools to dew point, further cooling causes condensation.

The relative humidity, usually abbreviated as RH, is the amount of water vapour actually present in air expressed as a percentage of the maximum possible at that temperature. When the RH is high, then comparatively little cooling of the air will lower temperature to dew point and produce condensation. When the relative humidity is low, temperature can fall a long way before any condensation occurs.

Evaporation is the reverse process by which air transforms condensation back again into invisible vapour once temperature rises again above dew point. The process requires the use of heat which is obtained either from the air itself, causing a momentary fall in temperature of the immediate environment, or from the surface on which the water drops are lying. The most familiar example of this is the thermostatic control system of the human body, which maintains normal temperature in hot weather by the evaporation of sweat. The principle is used in order to measure the relative humidity and dew point of air.

A wet-and-dry bulb thermometer consists of two mercury thermometers mounted side by side, one of which has its bulb encased in muslin which is kept wet by a connecting wick dipped into a reservoir of distilled water. The wet bulb temperature is always lower than the dry bulb temperature when the air is clear and therefore below saturation vapour content, because evaporation of water from the muslin extracts heat from the wet bulb. The drier the air, the greater the evaporation rate and the further the wet bulb temperature falls below the dry bulb temperature. When air is saturated, in fog or cloud, no moisture can evaporate from the muslin and both thermometers read the same.

The dew point of air is approximately as far below the wet bulb temperature as the latter is below the dry bulb temperature. The exact figure, as well as relative humidity, is given in humidity tables which should always accompany any wet-and-dry thermometer. The nearer dew point is to the temperature of air, the greater the risk of condensation if air cools any more.

A whirling pyschrometer is a wet-and-dry bulb thermometer neatly packaged to look like a football match rattle and used in the same way — by whirling above the head! This ensures that evaporation takes place from the muslin to give a quick reading when required, and the instrument can meanwhile be kept within a dry cabin. An instrument mounted on the outside of a boat would often be invalidated by sea spray.

The key to forecasting all the wet weather phenomena lies in determining the dew point of air and any factor which might cause the temperature of air to fall below dew point. That is a gross oversimplification of the matter, but not because any

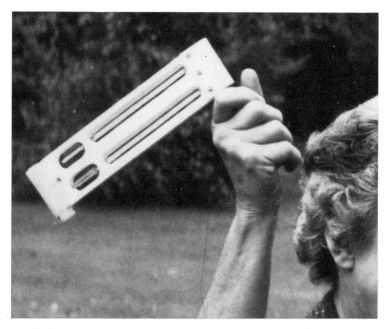

Whirling pyschrometer consisting of a wet and a dry bulb thermometer in a protective housing.

particular cooling factor is complicated. The trouble is that there are always several processes at work at the same time in a vast and non-homogenous atmosphere. Forecasting what will happen is never a neat arithmetical addition and subtraction of precise quantities, but it is surprising how weather-wise a yachtsman can become when he understands how each individual source of trouble arises.

Food for Thought
What is the raw material from which all wet weather is produced?
What is the dew point of air?
What causes condensation as dew, cloud, rain etc?
What is relative humidity?

6 Dew, frost and fog, by contact with cold surfaces

There are two ways by which air can cool because of contact with a cold surface. Either the air remains stationary and the surface itself radiates heat and cools, in which case condensation is called radiation dew or fog. Or, the air travels and reaches a surface already colder than the air, in which case condensation is called advection dew or fog. It is the same end product, but with adjectives describing the method of cooling involved.

Radiation of heat, by the Earth and everything upon it, is important at night when there is no Sun in the sky to dwarf its own relatively puny radiating efforts. So long as there is no cloud to intercept the radiated heat, surface temperatures may fall considerably. Obviously, cooling is particularly effective in winter when the nights are long; it is a factor to be reckoned with in spring and autumn; and it is least important in summer when the days are longer than the nights.

The air which lies close to any surface cools at the same time as the surface, and the resulting weather depends partly upon the strength of the wind. When there is a strong wind, every layer of air which cools near the ground gets quickly whipped away from that surface and into the moving airstream. Consequently, much more air cools but only a little. Providing that the air is fairly dry, temperature probably remains above dew point and the night stays fine.

Dew condenses from air when there is no wind and the cooling surface is level. Air close to it gets colder and colder as the surface cools progressively through the night, until air temperature reaches dew point, and dew forms; most readily on surfaces which cool rapidly (e.g. dry soil), on surfaces which are isolated from àny counteracting heat source (e.g. parked cars) and on surfaces which themselves provide additional water vapour to increase the relative humidity of the immediate environment (e.g. grass blades). The cabin top of a yacht in harbour collects dew, but less readily if the inside is heated and leaks heat through the hull. A moving yacht, however, creates its own wind which prevents air stagnating on the superstructure and cooling to dew point at all.

Dew *may* freeze to ice pellets when temperature subsequently falls to 0°C or below, but water drops can, and do, remain liquid when much colder and are then said to be supercooled.

Supercooled drops have a precarious existence because contact with solid substances or ice crystals cause them to solidify at once. In cloud however they can exist at temperatures down to −30°C.

Frost describes several meteorological conditions. *Air frost* means that air temperature at 4 ft above ground is 0°C or less; *ground frost* means that temperature close to the ground is sub-zero; *hoar frost* is condensation directly as ice crystals out of air, when the dew point is below 0°C.

There can be ground frost without air frost; there is usually ground frost when there is an air frost; but there can be an air frost without hoar frost if the air is dry and dew point well below 0°C.

Hoar frost on leaves. *M. J. Hammersley.*

Radiation fog results when the wind is just light enough to stir up the air *in situ*, rather than carry it vigorously away from cooling surfaces. Condensation then forms throughout a considerable thickness of air, perhaps several hundred feet. Mist patches close to the ground form first and then, as cooling continues, the mist thickens to impenetrable fog. Radiation fog forms most readily when air already has a high relative humidity at dusk, perhaps because it has travelled a long distance across the sea or because the ground is wet from recent rain. The banks of lakes and rivers are always more prone to fog than areas remote from water.

Mist clinging low to field after a still clear night. Tree tops are above the inversion level, in air warmer than the air near the ground.

Dew, frost and fog, being products of cooling dense air and very light wind, are particular risks in hollows and valleys, because the air drifts downhill under gravity.

Clearance of radiation fog begins when the Sun is high enough in the sky to evaporate the top of the fog layer, penetrate to the ground below and start the whole convective process by which air is warmed again. Sometimes radiation fog literally seems to disappear; at other times it lifts upwards to a thin layer of shapeless stratus, which later breaks into pancake shapes (called stratocumulus), veined with blue sky, before dispersing altogether. During the initial stirring of the air near the ground, hill tops which have been clear of fog during the night may become temporarily obscured by the clearing and rising fog.

Radiation fog has marked seasonal characteristics. In summer, if it forms at all, fog clears away very early in the morning. In spring and autumn, the Sun may not be strong enough to clear fog until mid-morning and it is then likely to re-form again in the early evening if the sky remains cloudless. Radiation fog which forms in the long nights of winter may persist for days on end until a more active weather system comes along. Radiation fog often occurs in persistent spells of high pressure when there is very little change in either wind or weather. Then it is worth remembering that fog formation and clearance get fixed into a fairly regular timetable. If it clears at about 11.30 a.m. and re-forms about 4.30 p.m. one day, then it is likely to do the same the next day, providing that there is no other change in overall conditions.

An inversion of temperature near the ground is the normal accompaniment to dew, frost or fog. This means that, instead of decreasing with height, temperature increases for a short height because of the intense cooling near the ground. Many a fruit farmer has reason to bless a shallow but intense inversion of temperature. Frost occurs at the base of a tree while temperature at blossom level is well above freezing point. In an urban context, ground floors of high rise buildings are sometimes shrouded in fog while the top floor has a clear view of the stars and enjoys a temperature several degrees higher than the street below.

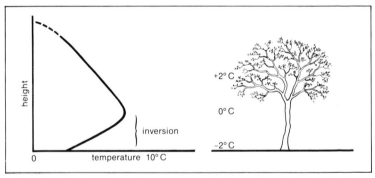

An inversion of temperature exists when air becomes warmer with increasing height above ground.

An inversion often keeps fruit blossom safe even when there is frost on the ground

Radiation fog spells hopeless weather for inland sailors because it implies calm or very light wind.

At sea, yachtsmen are not afflicted with radiation fog because the sea does not cool appreciably during one or even several nights. Fog may drift off the land on to the harbour or beach but it usually clears again over the warmer sea. Sea sailors do, however, suffer secondary effects from radiation fog over land, because it inhibits the development of a sea breeze.

Advection fog is the same nasty stuff as radiation fog but formed in a slightly different manner. Instead of calm air stagnating over a surface which is cooling, travelling air (i.e. wind) moves to a surface which is already colder than the dew

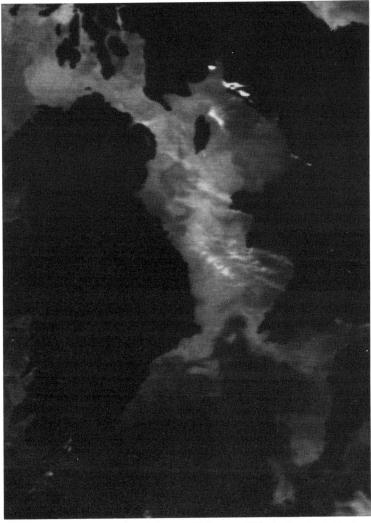

Infra-red picture of the Irish Sea on 20 August 1976, during the hottest summer of the century. The land is the hottest area, black, but the sea is much colder, with noticeable variations in temperatures. *Courtesy of Dundee University.*

point of air. The boundary may be abrupt, for instance when the wind changes to bring warm air to snowy or frost-bound land; fog is the usual precursor of thaw after a hard winter. At sea, too, there are cold currents which create abrupt temperature boundaries. The notorious fog banks off Newfoundland occur when mild air overruns the cold Labrador current; sea fog often swirls over the cold Pacific current off the coast of California. Watch for sea fog wherever there are currents which are particularly cold for their latitude because they are flowing away from the poles.

Sea fog also forms when air cools gradually by travelling into higher latitudes over a gradually cooling sea surface. Fog forms patchily at first, because the upwellings of water near the surface maintain slight inequalities of temperature. When the sea surface becomes consistently colder than the dew point of the air travelling across it, then fog thickens to a continuous blanket. It is particularly prevalent in early spring when the sea is coldest, but sea fog can form even in high summer. The sea is then relatively cold compared with the land, and wind having an appreciable sea track, for instance down the North Sea or along the English Channel, may cool and pick up enough additional moisture to form fog.

Anticipate a risk of sea fog whenever the isobars on a synoptic chart indicate that wind is blowing polewards and likely to arrive in a yachting area after a long fetch across the sea. Sea fog

Stratus (lifted sea fog) at Christchurch, New Zealand, blowing straight off the sea from right of picture, evaporating in the warmer conditions inland
M. J. Hammersley

Cadets sailing beneath a sheet of stratus.

can persist in winds up to about 10 knots because the long sea journey makes the lower air consistently moist. Whatever skin of air is lifted off the sea at one moment is replaced by another equally moist. If the wind is stronger than 10 knots, fog may get lifted above the surface to hang as a sheet of low formless cloud called stratus. Grey and dismal it may be, but at any rate it permits reasonable visibility and safe sailing.

When a risk of sea fog has been surmised from the isobaric chart a more accurate estimation can be made by estimating the dew point of air with a whirling psychrometer. Compare this with the temperature of the sea, hoisted by bucket from the surface, and if the two temperatures are nearly the same sea fog is a real threat.

Sea fog does not evaporate, even in summer, simply because the Sun rises. The sea remains cold and the wind continually brings a supply of near-saturated air to cool finally to dew point above its surface. Only a radical change in wind direction, bringing drier air, enables the sea fog to clear and it is usually beyond the powers of a yachtsman to predict when this will happen. In such a situation, pay careful attention to broadcast weather bulletins for every clue about further prospects.

It is sometimes possible for dinghy yachtsmen, who are able

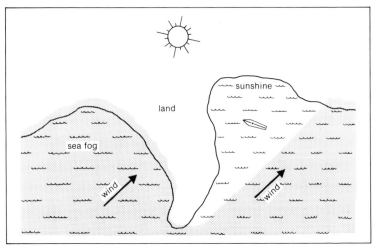

Sea fog may clear after a short passage across warming land in summer

to trail their boats to different waters, to evade sea fog altogether. Study a local map and search for a bay or estuary protected on the windward side by a headland. Quite a narrow strip of land, which is warming in the sunshine, may be sufficient to evaporate sea fog which drifts across it, so that bright weather prevails over the sea to leeward.

Food for Thought
What is the difference in the way radiation fog and advection fog are formed?
What difference does wind strength make to the risk of radiation fog?
What determines if condensation forms as dew or hoar frost?
What is the difference between the way radiation fog clears away and clearance of sea fog?
What is an inversion of temperature?
When is sea fog most likely?
Where would you look for sunshine in summer when sea fog blankets the shore?

7 Clouds and showers, by lift over high ground and in thermals

It is an adiabatic process which produces cloud and rain, and that daunting adjective has probably caused countless people to shut their text books in fright! The term loses much of its sting when translated from the original Greek language. *A* means *not*, *diabino* means *pass through*. Adiabatic therefore refers to the fact that the temperature of a volume of air may change without any heat either entering or leaving that volume. The temperature change is a self-contained conversion of work energy into heat energy, or vice versa.

Let me quote two examples, familiar to most people.

Air which is compressed through a bicycle pump into a tyre warms, even though no outside heat source is playing upon the pump.

Gas which expands when released from a cartridge into a soda syphon cools enough to make the cartridge uncomfortably cold to handle, even though it was at room temperature a moment before.

In the atmosphere, air may be forced for various reasons to sink or lift, and this alters the atmospheric pressure acting upon it. Air which sinks suffers an increase in atmospheric pressure and its temperature rises in consequence. Air which is lifted into regions of lower atmospheric pressure expands, and its temperature falls. Cooling by lift in different ways is the key to condensation as clouds, and rain, snow or hail.

Orographic lift is the forced ascent of an airstream which encounters the obstacle of a mountain or hill in its path. If the air is very moist it may cool to dew point even before reaching the top of the obstacle, clinging to the windward slope and obscuring the summit. Cloud clears again on the leeward side as the airstream sinks again and warms. The official name of such cloud is *stratus*, but it has many nicknames in localities where it is seen frequently. It may be Scotch mist in Scotland, mizzle in Devon and Cornwall, and has acquired fame as Table Cloth when hanging over Table Mountain outside Cape Town in South Africa. If you happen to be actually on the mountain top, then it becomes, more prosaically, hill fog. The lower the cloud

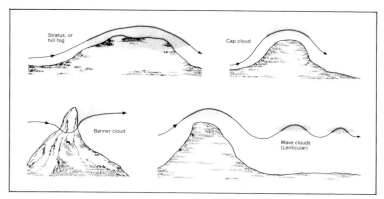

Orographic clouds, formed by expansion, cooling and condensation from air forced to lift over high ground

clings to the side of any mountain, the higher the relative humidity of the air, and the more important it becomes for a yachtsman on adjoining water to consider the risk of sea fog.

When the air is fairly dry, then a *cap* cloud may cover the peak of a mountain or sit just above it. Sometimes the cloud looks ragged and sometimes smoothly curved like a lens, but it always appears stationary, whatever the wind strength. This is because the cloud is not one particular conglomeration of water drops but a succession of drops which are condensed from the air on the windward side and evaporate again on the leeward side. The wind blows through the cloud instead of driving it along. Occasionally the airstream undulates in wave motion down wind and then small clouds may form in each crest, getting more insignificant as the wave motion dies out.

Banner clouds stream downwind from many famous pointed peaks. The air divides around the tip, eddying backwards and upwards to produce lift, so that a cloud clings to the lee side of the tip gradually evaporating as the turbulence ceases downwind. The Matterhorn in Switzerland, Mount Teide in the Canary Isles and Mount Fujiyama in Japan are among many which sport banner clouds which advertise that the air is too dry to shroud the mountain entirely but too moist to leave the tip entirely cloud free.

Thermal lift produces the shapely convection clouds, called *cumulus*, which vary from small fleeces dappling a blue sky to towering castles called *cumulonimbus* because they jettison showers. There are two stages to the production of a cumulus cloud.

1 Some heat source (usually the Sun) heats a surface (usually the

Fair weather cumulus, typical of a ridge of high pressure.

land) and causes the air above it to convect upwards. This continues until a powerful thermal current develops.

2 The air in the rising thermal is carried into regions of lower and lower atmospheric pressure, cooling adiabatically all the time.

Cloud base indicates the level at which air cools to dew point, and in the early morning, while there are still variations in

Large cumulus, typical of vigorous thermals in unstable airstream.

humidity near the ground, bases may be at different heights. By the time thermal activity has thoroughly stirred the lower atmosphere into a homogenous entity, bases often look as firm and level as if trimmed with knife and measuring rod. Such tidy cumulus are usually shallow and indicative of fine weather.

The top contour indicates the progress of the thermal. If the outline is crisp and billowing, the thermal is still rising and the cloud growing. When cumulus tops become blurred and flattened it shows that the thermal has reached the limit of its ascent. The cloud starts to evaporate in an adjacent downcurrent which is warming adiabatically, and another vigorous upcurrent creates another cumulus. Convection clouds are therefore telltale indicators of vertical motion in the atmosphere and this causes gustiness when superimposed upon the horizontal pressure gradient wind. The bigger the convection clouds, the more gusty the wind.

Cumulus travel on the horizontal pressure wind but they do not travel the world unchanged. When you look at the white-on-blue patchwork in the sky you are witnessing the actual production and destruction process itself. Cumulus are continually forming new leading edges and evaporating again in downcurrents.

Although the Sun is the principal heat source which triggers thermals and convection clouds, it is not the only one. Power station chimneys and burning stubble fields often emit enough

Cumulus with crisp tops developing over the distant shore. The land is a thermal source, but not the sea.

heat to become surmounted by shallow cumulus. Of more importance to yachtsmen, the sea, too, serves as a thermal source whenever the wind blowing across it is considerably colder. That means whenever an airstream of polar origin travels into lower latitudes, and in winter when very cold air off the land blows across sea which is relatively warm.

Cumulus over land are diurnal, following the rise and set of the Sun. Clouds start developing in the morning, build up to a maximum in the afternoon and disperse in the evening to leave a clear sky.

Cumulus over the sea, however, may persist day and night because the sea temperature does not change. If it is a thermal source by day it will also be a thermal source by night, unless other factors intervene. If the wind is on-shore, cumulus may drift off the sea and deprive coastal towns of their fine night too. **Cumulonimbus**, the biggest of the convection breed, give showers of rain or snow, and sometimes hail or thunder. Hailstones are drops of water which have been tossed up and down in powerful air currents within the cloud, freezing in the process till they are heavy enough to fall against the upthrusting air. The precise reason why cloud droplets amalgamate to fall as precipitation at all remains something of a puzzle and so do the exact reasons for thunder and lightning. For practical purposes it is enough to be able to recognize the appearance and consequences of a cumulonimbus, about which there is no doubt whatsoever.

Cumulonimbus seen in full depth, blowing along the coast from left to right of the picture. Anvil tops indicate the clouds which are on the wane; adjacent billowing cells still soaring upwards.

In maturity, a cumulonimbus has a billowing top like a giant cauliflower which is tall enough to be seen above most urban or mountainous obstructions on the immediate horizon. The upper part of the cloud has an intensely white colour which indicates that the constituent water drops, which can remain supercooled but liquid for many degrees below 0°C, are solidifying at last into ice crystals. This is called glaciation and is known to be pertinent in producing a shower. The base of a cumulonimbus is usually low, often with ragged patches of cloud below the main base, formed in the turbulent damp air. Sometimes a shower cloud has a black roll cloud along the leading edge, indicating a squall. Worse still, a cumulonimbus occasionally spawns a funnel cloud tapering down towards the ground from the main base, indicating a tornado on land or a water spout at sea.

The approach of any cumulonimbus should alert a yachtsman to prepare for violent fluctuations of both wind speed and direction. Updraughts of air into the leading edge of the cloud act rather like a giant suction machine, temporarily overpowering the surface wind on which a yacht has been sailing. This is the origin of the belief that a storm cloud 'comes up against the wind', which is a dangerous maxim if it encourages you to think that the threat will magically disappear the other way again. A cumulonimbus usually travels on the wind at about 10,000'; it is the yachtsman's surface wind which changes as the cloud gets near, blowing towards the leading edge. The shower falls with a downblast of cold air from the centre of the cloud and squally conditions prevail while the storm passes.

A cumulonimbus which is on the wane is often topped by dense white ice crystals shaped like an anvil. The water drops making up the lower part of the cloud evaporate in subsiding downcurrents but the ice crystal top persists longer, streaming along in the upper winds. Since these are usually stronger with increased height, the cloud gets drawn out into the typical anvil shape. After a showery day, the sky may be covered with residual ice cloud, called *cirrus*, from the tops of many cumulonimbus long after the rest of the clouds have disappeared.

A shower, in meteorological language, relates specifically to the precipitation from cumulonimbus. It may be torrential or little more than a few drops, but it is always short lived; usually considerably less than an hour, sometimes only a few minutes. Occasionally, however, cumulonimbus follow each other in quick succession so that a sequence of showers makes it seem that it has been raining for hours. The word *showers* will still be used, however, because it also informs that the precipitation is falling from cumulonimbus clouds.

The size of cumulus clouds, shallow and innocuous, or deep and violent, depends upon the buoyancy of rising air within the environment. Air continues to rise so long as it is warmer and therefore lighter than its surroundings, but comes to a halt once it is colder than its surroundings. That level marks the top of cloud.

The atmosphere overhead has a unique profile (graph of temperature with altitude) every day, which meteorologists obtain by radio sonde instruments sent up on balloons. Generally speaking, air gets colder with height, but sometimes temperature remains constant, even increases, with height within a shallow layer. Origin and past history of the air determines the profile, which is never a smooth curve and sometime much steeper than other times.

A rising thermal of air, on the other hand, is a relatively small scale and short lived phenomenon which behaves independently within the environment, cooling at known rates as if in a laboratory experiment. Clear unsaturated air cools at 3°C per 1000 ft rise into the atmosphere, but once it reaches dew point and forms a cloud base, cools within cloud at a lesser saturated rate. It is a lesser rate because the process of condensation releases latent heat which counteracts the cooling due to expansion under reduced pressure. On average the saturated lapse rate is 2°C but it varies according to the amount of vapour available for condensation. The saturated lapse rate curve is smooth and its intersection with the temperature profile of the

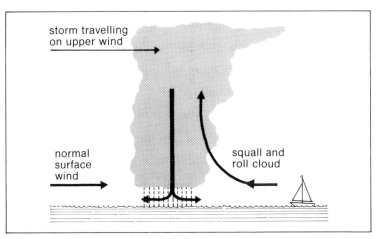

Surface wind is sucked towards the leading edge of an approaching storm, becomes particularly violent and changeable near the squall line, and may change yet again in the downblast of cold air and precipitaion from the centre of the cloud.

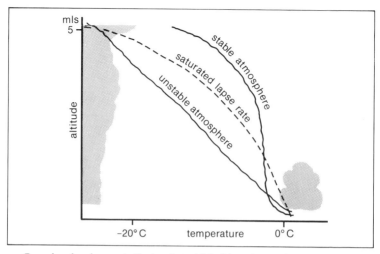

Cumulus develop up to the level at which rising air in a thermal becomes colder than its surroundings. This occurs sooner in stable air than in unstable air.

environment marks the limit of convection. Beyond that point rising air becomes colder than its surroundings and non-buoyant.

The upper air charts illustrated are simplified versions of those used by meteorologists and show how the slope of the environment curve determines the size of cumulus clouds. The steeper profile intersects the lapse rate curve at a low altitude, cumulus remain small and the atmosphere is said to be *stable.* The flatter curve, however, does not intersect the lapse rate curve of the rising air until several miles high, so that large cumulus develop in the *unstable air.*

Upper air charts are not available to the general public, but the picture of pressure, wind and origin of air is shown on isobaric charts published in newspapers, shown on television or drawn oneself from the Shipping Bulletins. Air which is disproportionately cold aloft because blowing into lower latitudes and warming from the ground upwards has a flat temperature profile. Steep profiles show air which is warmer than usual aloft, either because originating in warmer latitudes and cooling in the lower layers when travelling, or because upper air is subsiding and warming by compression because of divergent surface winds around high pressure. A glance at the isobaric pattern each day will soon make you familiar with those which predict showers and those which don't.

Surface wind is usually gusty in unstable conditions. Thermal upcurrents into cumulus clouds detract from the strength of the pressure gradient wind and result in lulls, while the downcurrents bring to the surface air which has been blowing faster without the drag of surface friction. Momentarily these downcurrents retain there upper air identity and a yacht experiences gusts akin to the direction and strength given by the isobars for 2000'. Be constantly alert to gust-lull conditions, especially by watching wind movements on the sea surface. Cumulus clouds travel on the wind, and some thermals actually slope according to the increasing wind speed with height. Gusts and lulls, therefore do not always occur in tidy fashion beneath clouds and clear air.

At night overland, wind steadies and speed falls much lighter. Over the sea, gusty wind may prevail at night if that has been the condition the previous day.

Visibility is usually excellent in unstable air, except actually in showers, because dirt from the many pollution sources convects quickly in thermals into the upper atmosphere. With the Sun shining and good visibility, the weather-wise decide, correctly, that it is 'too good to last', because cumulus development and showers cause weather to deteriorate quickly.

When the atmosphere is stable and cumulus clouds are small then dirt remains trapped much nearer the ground and visibility remains poor with haze obscuring the sky.

Food for Thought

What happens to the temperature of air a) when compressed b) when allowed to expand?

What happens when air is forced to surmount high ground?

What are the two separate processes which result in convection cloud?

How can you tell by looking at a cumulus cloud if it is continuing to grow upwards, or dispersing?

What effect do cumulus clouds have on wind?

What are the particular hazards of an approaching cumulonimbus upon the winds affecting a yacht?

Name 3 kinds of precipitation which can fall from a cumulonimbus?

Is unstable air disproportionately cold aloft or warm aloft?

In what kind of pressure system would you expect stable air?

What difference in visibility might indicate deep convection clouds or shallow ones?

8 Clouds, rain and snow, by lift in converging winds

Convergence of contrasting air streams is a source of persistent lift because the two constituents cannot mix together at once — that takes time. Therefore, the colder, more dense, air undercuts the warmer which must rise in order to get out of the way. A boundary between such conflicting airs is appropriately called a front, and the battlefields of convergence are responsible for most of our bad weather.

A sea breeze front is a shallow convergence zone between cold air blowing on-shore in a sea breeze and opposing warm air over land blowing in an off-shore direction. The cold sea air undercuts the warm air and forces it to rise. If there are already cumulus clouds over land, then the sea breeze front will

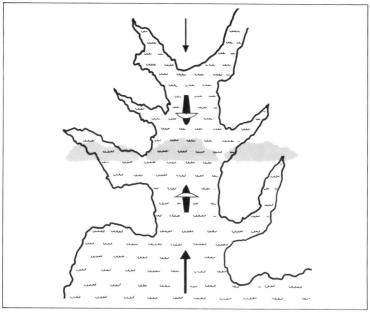

A sea breeze front is a line of cloud marking opposing sea breeze and pressure wind.

produce even larger clouds. If the day has been cloudless, the front will be marked by a noticeable line of cumulus. Usually the sea breeze is the stronger so that the sea breeze front lies over the land and can be driven quite a distance inland. But when it advances down a river estuary, a sailing scene can take a curious looking glass appearance. Either side of the sea breeze front yachts may have their sails set for wind astern, yet all yachts are converging towards each other!

A cold front is the boundary, at ground level, between deep cold air and warmer air which it is undercutting. It is similar to a sea breeze front but on a grander scale, because the confronting air masses may have very different characteristics up to great heights. The cold dense air thrusts beneath the warm air with such vigour that it triggers off huge cumulonimbus, with all their attendant violence; showers, perhaps hail and thunder and very squally winds. Mercifully a cold front usually moves

A cold front disappearing in the distance, after giving a short-lived but torrential downpour.

quickly and passes through an area in well under an hour, but it may arrive at any time, day or night. A cold front has one redeeming characteristic over the random cumulonimbus of a showery day — it is usually such a pronounced feature that it

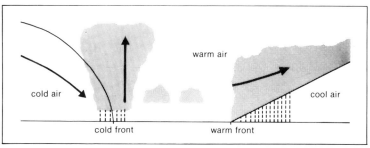

Vertical cross section through a cold and warm front. Cirrus, cloud first visible 300-500 miles ahead of warm front.

can be tracked on a weather map, thus reducing somewhat the element of surprise. A cold front is drawn on a weather map either as a blue line, or as a black line with jagged teeth on the side towards which it is advancing. It is 'drawn' just as clearly in the sky so that satellites photograph it as a white curve of cloud several hundred miles long.

The yachtsman gets only a midget's view of the giant. First of all angry black cloud bearing down on him from windward; then the wildly fluctuating wind and the storm itself; then a dramatic change to bright sunshine behind the front, with the line of towering cumulus downwind dividing the sky into clear and cloudy halves. The brighter weather is accompanied by a noticeable fall in air temperature and cumulus may then develop in the cold air if it travels across warmer surfaces.

A cold front moves at the speed of the pressure gradient wind pushing behind it, provided that the wind impinges at right angles to the line of the front. If the pressure wind blows at an angle to the front, then only one component of the wind, that at right angles to the front, is useful in pushing the front along. A front is stationary when the pressure wind blows parallel to it. **A warm front** is the boundary at ground level between warm air and cooler air downwind over which it is being forced to ascend by pursuing cold air. Clouds heralding a warm front appear several hundred miles downwind, visible simply because of their elevation in the sky.

Feathery plumes of ice crystal cloud, called *cirrus*, appear first and gradually blend into a continuous veil of *cirrostratus* covering the whole sky. The Sun is dimmed, thermal activity ceases and cumulus disperse. At night, the ice crystal cloud is detectable by a halo around the moon caused by the refraction of light passing through. A halo always has red on the inside, with faint yellow and blue outside. (A corona, sometimes seen through thin sheets of water drop cloud, has red on the outside and no significance for predicting the advance of a warm front.)

Cirrus gradually thickens to formless grey cloud, called *altostratus* obscuring the Sun completely and giving rain (or snow in winter). Rain may be light or heavy according to the vigour of the front but it usually lasts for several hours, during which time low cloud called *nimbo stratus*, forms in the turbulent moist airstream below the altostratus. A typical rain belt from an active warm front lasts 4-6 hours, which has created the belief 'rain before seven, fine before eleven'. It is a reasonable maxim as far as the period of 4 hours is concerned but there is no significance to the hours of seven and eleven, which are merely convenient rhyming words. A warm front, like a cold front, travels by night or day.

Cirrus tufts consolidating into a film of cirrostratus and thickening on the
horizon to altostratus, indicating approach of warm front
M. J. Hammersley

Altrostratus blurring the Sun and darkening towards the horizon — rain
very soon.

Behind the warm front, rain stops and cloud clears away, while air temperature often rises noticeably. During the day small fair weather cumulus develop in summer over the land; in winter both day and night, fog or low stratus is a risk as warm air cools over colder surfaces.

A warm front is drawn on a weather chart as a red line, or as a black line adorned with semicircles on the side towards which it is advancing. It travels at about ⅔ the speed of the pressure wind pushing it from the rear, which is slower than a cold front would move with the same wind. Hence a cold front often catches up with a warm front after both have been in existence for a day or so, and the fronts are then said to be occluded. **An occlusion** is the surface boundary between the air behind a cold front and the air ahead of the warm front. The warm air itself gets squeezed upwards right off the ground, so that no marked rise in air temperature is noticed on the ground. The cloud sequence remains the same but without any fair weather break between the warm front rain and the downpour from

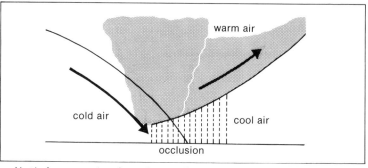

Vertical cross section through an occlusion

cumulonimbus at the cold front. An occlusion is usually an indication that the original fronts are a few days old and their distinctive boundaries are becoming mixed and blurred. The whole front may disperse into patchy altostratus without rain, but any new infusion of contrasting air may resurrect an old occlusion.

There are two major convergence zones in each hemisphere. Near the equator, where the north-east and south-east trade winds of the two hemispheres converge, considerable cloud forms even though the air masses are usually similar. In the temperate latitudes, 40°-70°N or S, more pronounced confrontations occur between cold and warm air blowing around the high

pressure circulations at the poles and in the subtropics. These polar fronts behave in fluid fashion and form waves with crests

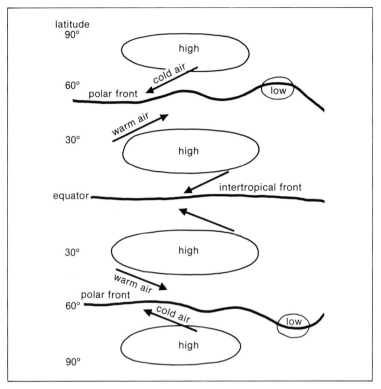

Major fronts around the world

on the poleward sides. Atmospheric pressure falls at each tip and a complete circulation of air, called a depression, develops. In the waving process a sector of warm air gets trapped in a squeeze between fresh cold air behind the depression and the degenerate cool air ahead. Two fronts are born and travel along with the depression.

Food for Thought
What is a sea breeze front?
What are the characteristics of cold front weather?
What is the cloud sequence observed in the sky when a warm front is approaching?
When do warm and cold fronts usually arrive, by day or night?
What happens when a cold front catches up with a warm front?
In which latitudes do the travelling depressions roam?
What is the Polar Front?

Overleaf: Sea fog and sunshine can be close neighbours; a short journey across warming land often clears fog in summer.

Sea fog lying below a sunny cliff top, with island beyond also standing above fog.

Stratus cloud, lifted fog, breaking up into diffuse patches and about to disperse altogether.

9 Isobars around low pressure

Having explained how different clouds form, it is time to link their occurrence with isobars and weather charts, by which meteorologists convey what is happening.

Hurricanes and tropical storms are the most violent of low pressure systems, and were familiar to sailors long before the connection between pressure and wind was understood. Sailors described the circular wall of towering clouds, the cloudless and relatively calm 'eye' of the storm and the manner in which the furious wind whirled around the eye; anticlockwise in the northern hemisphere and clockwise in the southern. They recognized, too, that the relative calm in the eye was only a temporary lull before the wind reasserted itself from the opposite direction and that the storms generally travelled towards the west before re-curving eastward into higher latitudes.

A Law of Storms was published in 1838 by Colonel William Reid, Scottish soldier and later colonial governor, which gave guidance about the evasive action ships should take if in the vicinity. Briefly the most dangerous quadrant of the storm was the forward quadrant on the poleward side, because any ship running before the wind would be carried into the path of the storm and towards the strongest winds. The navigable semicircle was the semicircle on the equator side of the storm where a ship running before the wind would be moving from trouble. The rotating storms were called hurricanes in the Atlantic and typhoons in the Pacific, but there were many local variations on these names.

The increasing use of barometers in ships soon provided proof that the centres of hurricanes invariably had exceptionally low pressure. Since the storms travelled, rapidly falling pressure was a sure sign of an approaching hurricane, and an equally rapid rise of pressure showed that it was departing. In 1848 tropical storms acquired the general name of cyclone. To-day, the name *cyclone* is reserved for intense tropical low pressure systems which do not attain hurricane strength winds, and *hurricanes* are those which have a mean wind speed over 64

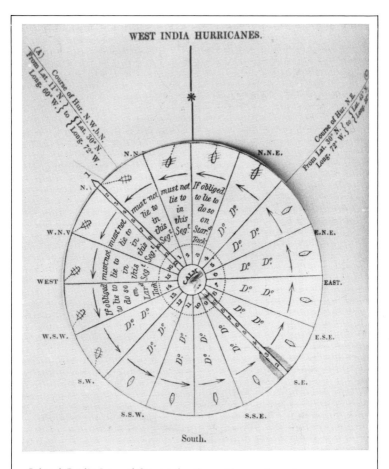

Colonel Reid's Law of Storms for the guidance of mariners.

1. The thin black lines represent the courses of the Hurricanes.
2. The long arrow through the centre of the circle is the projection of the course of the Hurricane.
3. The small ships have their heads turned in directions towards positions of greatest safety.
4. The small arrows are the direction of the wind (flying *with* it) in different parts of the hurricane. It will be noticed that the West India Hurricanes being north of the Equator revolve in an opposite direction to East India Hurricanes which are South of it.
5. The letter press in the segments are directions for lying to.
6. The numbers arranged round the centre are the numbers of the segments and serve to connect the diagrams with the tables.
7. The numbers in the long arrows are the depressions in tenths of inches of the Barometer, and are true (nearly) for all parts of the Hurricane at the same distance from the vortex.

A banner cloud streaming from the Matterhorn, Switzerland. *F Ross*.

Temporary cloud formed in an anabatic (upslope) wind in early morning on the Isle of Capri.

Smooth topped clouds formed in orographic life over high ground.

knots. Hurricanes feed upon the warmth and moisture of tropical seas and are most frequent in late summer and early autumn when the water is warmest. Once hurricanes reach land they usually degenerate into depressions, whose wind speeds are less but whose precipitation is often intensified by lift of air over the land.

Buys Ballot proved that *all* winds blow as circulations around high or low pressure centres, and the latter obey the same rules as the Law of Storms. Low pressure systems of temperate latitudes are called depressions, and are less violent than hurricanes but cover greater areas. Nevertheless, depressions often develop winds which are crippling to yachtsmen.

Surface wind converges towards the centre of all depressions, forcing air near the centre to rise in order to make room for the net inflow. This accentuates any other lift factor which produces cloud and accounts for the bad weather associated with low pressure. Convergence is most pronounced where the isobars conform to a small radius, which means around the centre of a depression or at the end of a *trough*, which is an elongation of the isobars away from the centre.

Isobars have real and fictional aspects. They really do portray atmospheric pressure and wind direction, but each particular isobaric chart is only one still picture captured from a continually changing series of lines. There are no actual tramlines in the sky which force the same air mass to circulate round and round without altering. A depression pattern may look the same after a journey of several hundred miles but the air in the circulation has been modified on the journey by new air streams infiltrating from all sides. In the rear of a depression even a slight curvature of the isobars indicate a convergence of airs which are dissimilar enough to produce a line of cumulonimbus clouds akin to a front. In a well-marked trough of low pressure, wind direction may be almost 180° different on either side and there is no way that an air mass can turn that sort of corner. What you see on the chart is a convergence zone of two different airs.

Depressions are born, reach maturity and then decline and die; they travel in their youth and stagnate in their retirement; some are feeble from birth and never make a mark upon the world, while others attain a vigour which makes them remembered with as much awe as a hurricane. In fact, they often do attain wind speeds of hurricane intensity, but rarely for sustained periods. The birthplace of depressions is important, because if it is a long distance away the growth can be monitored by satellite and synoptic observations so that their future intensity and position can be included in any forecast

The Fastnet storm approaching Ireland 1537 GMT on 13 August 1979.
The alignment of clouds, ahead and behind the cold front, indicate the
wind changes which created such enormous seas (Tiros-N,Vis).
Courtesy of Dundee University.

Large cumulus over land, with anvil top behind.

A street of shallow cumulus, typical of high pressure weather, blowing downwind from some thermal source.

Squall line at the leading edge of a cumulonimbus. *M J Hammersley.*

published or broadcast by a meteorological office. Most of the depressions which affect Great Britain are of this nature, forming on the polar front in the Atlantic and approaching Europe as mature specimens. There are, however, depressions which form on one's own doorstep and then it is impossible for even a meteorological office to pinpoint their centre and disposition until they have developed sufficiently to provide visible symptoms. By that time a yachtsman may be on the borders of trouble and must be able to recognize it and act on his own initiative.

Depressions travel generally eastward because of the spin of the Earth, but each takes a route of its choice towards some easterly point of the compass. During its active life a depression usually has two associated fronts which travel with it, the cold front faster than the warm front. The two fronts contain a warm sector within their boundaries which is lifted above the ground once the fronts become occluded. A depression usually travels in the direction of the wind in the warm sector, and speed of travel varies with the intensity of the system. A relatively small depression of a few hundred miles diameter which is deepening (i.e. whose central pressure is still falling) may travel at 30-40 knots. It may bring gale winds and be thoroughly unpleasant but it passes quickly and its future positions can usually be forecast reasonably accurately by extrapolation on a weather chart. Even so, the number of times in a weather forecaster's life when he can say 'the cold front will pass through at 11.5 a.m.' and behold, it does, can be counted on the fingers of one hand. Depressions and their fronts may change course, deepen or fill, in quite unpredictable manner. Hence the importance of watching the tell-tale symptoms in the sky and on the barometer, to make sure they tally with the previous opinion expressed in a forecast, and making your own amendments if circumstances seem to warrant it.

Pressure movements, called tendency, give a vital clue to wind changes around a depression. Convince yourself by playing a game with the diagrams opposite.

Imagine yourself at X, in either hemisphere, and hold a finger stationary above the spot. Then move the page underneath your finger in the direction of the warm sector isobars, and note the values of the isobars passing beneath. Lower and lower as the warm front approaches, steady above the one isobar in the warm sector, rising values behind the cold front. Do the same with your finger above Y, which is in the direct path of the depression. More isobars pass beneath your finger, indicating that pressure falls and rises most near the centre of depressions than on the periphery. The depression may be advancing

Typical active depressions with associated fronts

Northern hemisphere

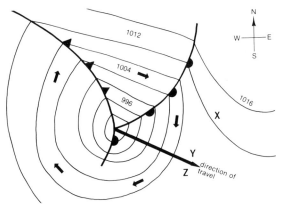

South of the centre, the wind *backs* from the direction it was blowing in the previous ridge of high pressure, as the depression and warm front advance; *veers* as the warm front passes; *veers* again, usually very noticeably, as the cold front passes.

North of the centre, the wind *backs all the time* that the depression advances and moves across an area, until the wind eventually becomes the same, in the rear of the depression, as that experienced by a yacht which was south of the centre.

Southern hemisphere

North of the centre, wind *veers* from the direction it was blowing in the previous ridge of high pressure, as the depression and warm front advance; *backs* as the warm front passes; *backs* again, usually very noticeably, as the cold front passes.

South of the centre, the wind *veers all the time* that the depression advances and moves across an area, until the wind eventually becomes the same, in the rear of the depression, as that experienced by a yacht which was north of the centre.

Cirrus, thickening to altostratus on the horizon, ahead of an approaching warm front. *M J Hammersley*.

Sun almost obscured by altostratus ahead of a warm front. Rain likely soon.

High stratocumulus, formed in early morning under inversion of temperature, breaking up to become a cloudless day with high pressure.

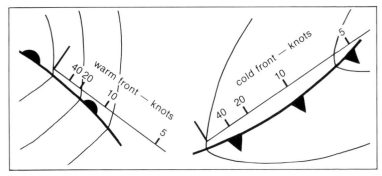

To measure the speed of fronts, place the appropriate scale so that the highest value sits over one isobar. The reading at the next isobar intersection gives the speed of front.

without deepening, but if pressure falls are rapid the depression is probably both advancing and deepening, often heralding gales.

Tendency values shown on your yacht's barometer give a useful warning of bad weather. 8 mb fall in 3 hours is an almost certain indication of gale, and 5 mb in 3 hours warning of force 6 wind. However, the story given by *one* barometer cannot determine a pressure gradient, at least two readings are needed from places some distance apart. An obstinate anticyclone may be holding its own against an advancing depression; steady pressure on your barometer can then give no absolute assurance that there will *not* be gales.

The manner of wind direction changes, as a depression passes across a yachting area, can be vitally important in assessing which are likely to be dangerous lee shores. The position of the yacht relative to the centre of the depression makes all the difference to whether wind changes by veering or by backing. Play the finger game once more with the isobaric charts, including also yacht position Z, and confirm the rules of change given in the captions.

The speed of fronts can be gauged with a geostrophic scale printed on blank weather maps. Place the highest value of the appropriate scale on the intersection of one isobar with the front, lay the scale along the line of the front itself and read the speed of the front by the point where the next isobar cuts the scale. The more widely spaced the isobars in the region under investigation, the slower the front will be moving, and quite often there is no second isobar close enough to the first to get a reading at all. The front is then stationary, and may be a potential source of a fresh depression.

'**Variable cyclonic**' is a forecasting term which should make you particularly alert. It means that the centre of the depression is expected right through the area concerned, so that your wind may change direction in either manner and possibly with rapidity. If it is an intense depression, wind speed may be strong too. Listen to every radio forecast for further information about the progress of the depression.

A secondary depression often develops when a depression is on the wane. The associated occlusion or cold front may trail behind, having travelled faster near the centre than further away, and the isobars are stretched into an elongated trough. It is a pressure pattern to watch carefully, as improbable in fluid terms as an elongated drop of water hanging from a dripping

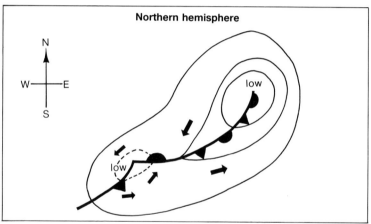

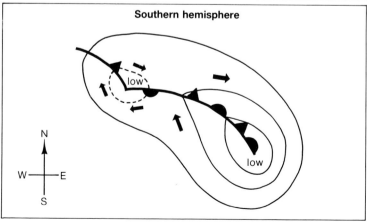

Typical low pressure pattern which breeds a secondary depression.

tap. You know the water must fall as a separate drop from the tap and you must likewise be alert for a secondary depression to form on the trailing front. The trough is a convergence zone of contrasting winds, sometimes almost 180° different on either side, and the old front gets renewed by further inflow of vigorous air.

Do not let the word 'secondary' lull you into thinking that such a depression is necessarily second rate, because it often develops into a worse tyrant than its parent. Gales are particularly likely if pressure falls fast and if the depression funnels between two land masses, such as the English and the French coasts. The Atlantic approaches to the English Channel is a favourite breeding ground for secondary depressions and holds bitter memories for many yachtsmen.

Families of depressions often travel in succession, with brief ridges of high pressure in between giving short spells of fine weather. There is no particular diurnal rhythm to the alternating wet and fine weather of an unsettled spell, but there is often some periodicity worth watching for. Sometimes wet days follow fine nights, at other times sunny days alternate with wet nights. But the interval between depressions is not always so brief and a 24 hour alternation is more usual. A rapid rise in pressure behind a depression is likely to herald only a temporary ridge of high pressure before the next low pressure system. Slow, steady, rise for several days is what foretells a longer lasting circulation around high pressure.

The decline of a depression is marked by rising pressure, faster near the centre than at the boundaries, which is called 'filling in'. The pressure gradient slackens, wind decreases and the depression loses its momentum. Some depressions then disappear from the weather chart, others stagnate as stationary depressions, having little wind but enough lift by convergence to squeeze continuous rain out of the atmosphere for perhaps several days. These are responsible for more floods than the fast moving depressions.

Tornadoes (over land) **and water spouts** (over the sea) are intense low pressure vortices sometimes bred within hurricanes, deep depressions or cumulonimbus. They are visible by funnel shaped clouds which lower from the main bases of storm clouds, but are too small and transient features to appear on synoptic charts. Pressure at the centre is exceptionally low and because the cross section is so small the pressure gradient is very steep. The fall in pressure occurs so quickly that it cannot equalise fast enough with the pressure inside closed buildings, which burst. The most destructive tornadoes occur over large tracts of land heated sufficiently to produce summer thunderstorms, and those of North America are notorious for their violence and frequency. Less spectacular tornadoes occur in Great Britain but even they cause a considerable trail of damage. Water spouts are liable to occur whenever there is vigorous convection and large cumulonimbus over the sea, but fortunately they are not as devastating as tornadoes.

Thermal lows form in a homogenous air mass, as distinct from depressions which form at the clash between two different air masses. When surface air is heated intensely it becomes less dense and pressure falls, sometimes enough to produce a quite distinct circulation. In summer over the land a shallow thermal low is a further development of the sea breeze effect. Over a relatively small area, such as the Midlands of England, sea breezes converge from all directions towards the middle of the land mass and air is persistently rising over the centre. It doesnt't rise far in what is usually the stable air of a heat wave, and the tenuous circulation often disappears again from the weather chart during the night. Over a huge land mass like India, however, where solar heating is much more intense, the

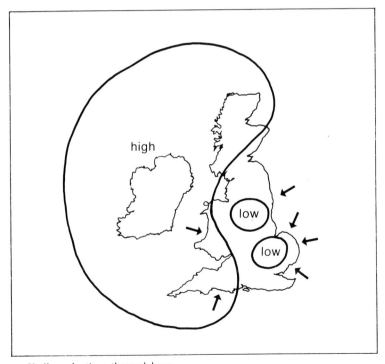

Shallow daytime thermal lows

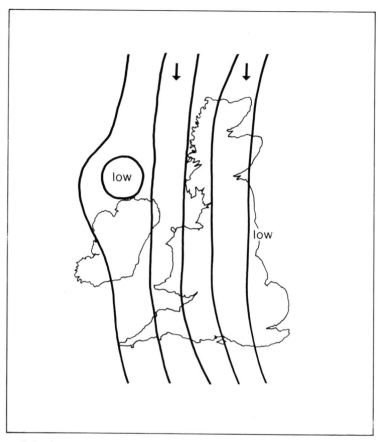

Polar low

thermal low does not disappear during the night but steadily builds up great depths into the atmosphere, wringing out the monsoon rain which persists for several months.

Polar lows are also thermal lows but with a different name to distinguish them from the summer variety. They occur when very cold air moves equatorwards over much warmer sea. The thermal stimulus is not so great as it can be over land in summer, but it is made more effective because the upper air is so cold and the atmosphere therefore unstable. These little lows often brew up quite nasty winds and showers, and once formed may remain on the weather chart for some time, travelling slowly within the air stream. They are most likely in winter when there is maximum contrast between polar air and the warmer sea of temperate latitudes.

Food for Thought

How does pressure change when a depression approaches?

What wind speed is implied by hurricane strength?

What is convergence, and why does it make weather deteriorate?

In which general direction do most depressions travel?

How does wind direction change if a depression passes when you are a) north of the centre b) south of the centre, in your own hemisphere?

What pressure pattern would make you suspect development of a secondary depression?

What time of year might you expect to find a thermal low on a weather chart?

10 Isobars around high pressure

Anticyclone is the name given to a high pressure circulation because it is so different, indeed opposite, to a cyclone. The isobars are usually widely spaced indicating light wind, which blow clockwise in the northern hemisphere and anticlockwise in the southern. The pressure pattern is roughly circular or oval,

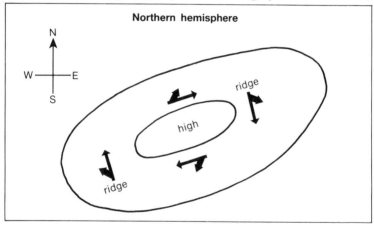

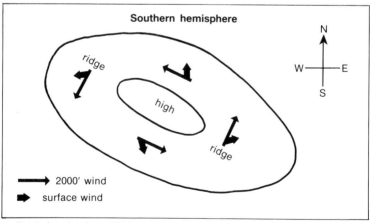

Typical anticyclone. High pressure pattern with wind blowing clockwise in the northern hemisphere and anticlockwise in the southern.

with the highest value covering more of a plateau area than a point centre. Anticyclones drift, rather than travel with measurable speed, and produce sluggish rather than vigorous weather. Cells of high pressure girdle the Earth around the sub-tropics, and extensions from these, called ridges, occasionally build up to mature anticyclones in the temperate latitudes. High pressure also develops over large continents in winter when there is intense cooling of the land and dense cold air. Ridges of high pressure extending from the Siberian anticyclone are notorious for bringing exceedingly cold weather to western Europe.

Subsidence of air is the key to high pressure weather. Surface wind diverges from the centre, upper air subsides to replace the net outflow of air below, thereby warming by compression and increasing its capacity for water vapour. Consequently, evaporation nibbles away the tops of cumulus clouds, which become blurred, and the clouds get shallower each day. Thermals continue to maintain crisp looking bases to cumulus until subsidence limits them so much that the air can no longer soar high enough to cool to dew point. The day becomes cloudless.

A ridge of high pressure usually occurs between one depression and another, so that subsidence often ensures that shower activity decreases after the first unstable day behind a cold front. However, the ridge is unlikely to develop into a mature anticyclone unless pressure rises slowly and persistently for several days.

Winter weather is liable to deteriorate after the first day or two of clear skies, because more heat is radiated at night than can be counteracted by the Sun next day. Each subsequent day becomes colder than the last, with relative humidity crucial in determining weather. If the air is dry, night-time temperatures have to fall very far before reaching dew point, so that weather remains cloudless but very cold and usually frosty.

If the wind brings moist air, however, even one night with cloudless skies may cool air to dew point and produce fog. Quickest near moist places like rivers or lakes, and in hollows to which cold air drains; even over the sea as well if the sea temperature is near its spring minimum temperature. When the wind is more than 10 knots condensation may be lifted off the ground as low cloud called stratus, cloaking the country in well named 'anticyclonic gloom', but at any rate maintaining reasonable visibility for land and sea traffic.

Neither fog nor stratus clear in winter until there is a radical change in wind.

High pressure weather in summer turns into heat waves. Day after day heat from the Sun accumulates, and radiation from the Earth at night does little to offset. Temperatures rise until eventually the hot air below the upper air inversion breaks through into the unstable layer above. Then weird turrets of convection cloud, called *castellanus*, build up rapidly with tops seen looming indistinctly high in the sky but with bases shrouded in the haze below.

Castellanus clouds produce thunderstorms, each convection cell being short lived but quickly followed by another in the vigorous see-sawing of the upper air. The impression given is of one long thunderstorm moving round and round, but in reality it is a succession of storms travelling little in the light upper winds. (These storms are different, therefore, from the short lived thunderstorms in shower clouds which blow past briskly in air streams which are unstable from the ground upwards.)

Cumulus castellanus over mountains shooting upwards in a manner indicating very unstable air. Probable thunderstorms by evening.

Thunderstorms may merely interrupt a heat wave, in which case pressure starts to rise again and the heat wave is renewed. But often the anticyclone declines after the storms, giving way to a low pressure pattern.

Heat wave storms mostly occur in the evening after another hot day has proved the last straw for an atmosphere supercharged with warm moist air. They also drift on the wind from elsewhere, arriving in the early morning as released energy from someone else's heat wave. In Great Britain, they often arrive on southeasterly winds from the larger land mass of Europe.

Thunder head looming above the haze, giving violent storm inland.

Wind in an anticyclone is usually light and variable and often hopeless for sailing in the winter. In summer the sea breeze is often the main wind at sea, but inland sailors get precious little.

If there is a little pressure wind, then inland sailors get very smooth sailing in the stable air, but at sea there may be considerable gustiness if cold air warms across warmer sea.

Visibility usually starts to deteriorate as soon as a ridge of high pressure develops into an anticyclone, and it gets worse as the high pressure persists, which may be for days or even weeks. Subsiding air aloft creates an inversion in the temperature profile of the atmosphere and this gets lower as the subsidence of air continues. Dirt in the lower levels of air remains trapped below the inversion, masking the blue sky with a white haze which may become threateningly black downwind of industrial areas. In winter, an ominous sky during high pressure rarely threatens a storm but it does give evidence of increased fog risk. Condensation is always facilitated by nucleii on which to form and a dirty atmosphere turns a relatively harmless fog into lethal smog.

A col is the no-man's-land between two diametrically opposite depressions and two diametrically opposite anticyclones. Pressure in the col is uniform, nearly as high as the fringe isobars around the anticyclone, a little bit higher than the fringe isobars round the depressions. Wind is calm or light and variable, ready to swing one way or another according to which boundary pattern gains precedence.

Food for thought
What is an anticyclone?
Which way does wind blow around high pressure in your own hemisphere?
Why do cumulus clouds disappear in an anticyclone?
What are the unpleasant aspects of high pressure in winter?
What are castellanus clouds, and what do they produce?
What is the characteristic of visibility in high pressure weather?

11 Forecasting with modern technology

Forecasting is a professional job, but people do not have to become meteorologists in order to keep one pace ahead of the weather. It does help, however, to have some idea of how forecasters go about their task; they have many technological wonders to help them but there are limits to what instruments can do on their own.

Satellites have miraculously extended human eyesight to cover the whole world. Cloud pictures taken on visible wave length are similar to holiday snaps from our own cameras, only giving results in daylight. Infra-red pictures, however, are as clear when taken by night as by day, but their message relates to temperature. The coldest clouds, land or sea, appear white, and warmer surfaces look grey through to black. Any picture can be coded into colours so as to highlight sections required for study. Satellite pictures show incredible detail when processed as glossy enlargements; they show adequate detail for forecasters when transmitted by facsimile machine to weather offices, but are not so good when shown at third hand on television.

Sunsynchronous satellites pass over an area at approximately the same local time each day, overriding each Pole every two hours and covering the entire Equator twice a day. During each orbit, the Earth rotates beneath, so places in between Equator and Poles are imaged from different angles in three consecutive passes twice every 24 hours. Sunsynchronous satellites cruise about 500 miles above the Earth — considered quite low!

Geosynchronous satellites, on the other hand, orbit at the staggering height of 22,300 miles so as to remain stationary above the Equator relative to the ground below. Instruments scan the Earth, strip by strip in sequence, so that after correction for time lag a complete picture of the circular half globe below is built up. This takes about half an hour, and the process starts all over again, to give a time lapse sequence invaluable to the forecaster. The edges of these pictures are too distorted to be useful but with 5 satellites in position around the world (one over the Greenwich meridian) and with the sunsynchronous satellites as well, there is reasonable coverage everywhere.

View of the half world from Meteosat on 7 July 1979 on visible wave length. Note depression approaching Spain. *Courtesy of Dundee University.*

Satellite data, which includes temperature, humidity and pressure sensor material, as well as pictures, comprise present facts; and time lapse sequences are hindcasting, not forecasting. Sometimes weather systems advance in orderly fashion so that one can extrapolate from what *was* to what *will be*, but often they act apparently by whim. Satellite information, therefore, is an extra topping to all the other information collected and distributed through the World Meteorological Organisation, but it still needs an experienced meteorologist to interpret.

Powerful computers help a lot with forecasting. Already in the 1920s the British Meteorologist, L. F. Richardson, wove physics principles into mathematical formulae and started the pipedream of numerical forecasting. After the Second World War computers made these ideas possible and to-day they can process complicated thermodynamic equations in minutes.

But even equations cannot take account of every factor which affects weather, and computers only give answers when they are fed facts. It is only possible to collect a sample of facts from the infinite total in the whole atmosphere, and some even have to be estimated from known data elsewhere in order to get a symmetrical model of the atmosphere. Nevertheless, despite these imprecisions, forecast pressure charts for a few days ahead have proved more reliable when made by computer than when made by forecasters, and are now used all the time. Computers can also produce general forecasts for cloud, wind, temperature and rainfall, but the specific detail needed by the public is likely always to come from a human brain reasoning around evidence and drawing upon a fund of past experience. **Most local forecasters** to-day are well served by technology. Facsimile machines disgorge weather charts, predicted pressure patterns and upper air charts, originated at headquarters, and the lucky offices get satellite pictures too. Teleprinters chatter incessantly (behind closed door!) with the latest weather observations together with general forecasts by senior meteorologists about what they expect to happen.

With an already plotted chart in front of him, a forecaster pinpoints the centres of high and low pressure and positions the fronts according to the latest data from the teleprinter. The reasoning goes something like this: "Rain has stopped at X and the wind has veered and pressure steadied, but it's still raining at Y with pressure falling. The front is through X but not through Y". Dew point is a good clue, always higher in a warm sector than behind the cold front.

Having placed the fronts, the forecaster estimates their positions several hours ahead and the details of future weather, always remembering that this rarely travels unchanged from one place to another. It may intensify or die away, be affected by high ground or by the resistance from high pressure elsewhere, etc.

When there are no fronts approaching, or in, the area a forecaster must assemble the clues about convection clouds. Stable or unstable air, how deep will cumulus develop, with or without showers, rain or snow, with or without hail, accentuated by high ground? And what about the following night — clear or cloudy skies, light or fresh wind, high or low humidity, frost or fog? An endless detective puzzle with no clue too small to be neglected and with no precise answers.

The best results in forecasting are obtained when a user adds his own knowledge of local topography and weather peculiarities to the necessarily short forecasts issued by meteorologists. Much as one would like more space in the press and more time on the air for greater weather detail, there is a limit to the usefulness of more words. The human brain cannot assimilate long speeches as easily as it can a picture, and weather changes so quickly that wordy detail would be overtaken by changes in the weather itself. The best picture for a yachtsman at sea is an isobaric chart, however roughly drawn.

Food for Thought
What does the whitest area of an infra-red satellite picture portray?
How would you pinpoint the passage of an active front on your self-made weather chart?

12 Making your own weather chart

Needless to say, there are no printed isobaric charts delivered to the cabin door when you are at sea, so if you want one, and I have persuaded you that they can be useful, you must make you own. It is not difficult because the professional forecaster has already down the hard work of assembling and interpreting data from all over the world. He then feeds to you his conclusions in abbreviated form. Every nation has its own format for broadcasting weather information, but the essential detail is the same everywhere. Here I shall discuss the Shipping Bulletin broadcast by the BBC in Great Britain. No wave lengths are given, no times of broadcast, because they are details which change frequently and every yachtsman must be responsible for keeping up to date.

The only equipment necessary for making an adequate isobaric chart is a radio capable of receiving on the required wave length, black and red ballpoint pens, pencil and eraser, and a supply of blank maps specially printed for the purpose. Additional handy equipment, but not vital, are an alarm clock to remind you to listen at the right time and a tape machine to record the message, as a precaution against missing any of the information.

The blank maps should be printed in two sections, the left side tabulated so that you can write down the bulletin in the same order that the items are read out. The tabulation should be as compact as possible to save moving your hand over the paper unnecessarily. The map itself, on the right side, should outline also the sea areas mentioned in the forecast, and should have geostrophic scales for measuring the wind and progress of fronts. Some charts have a scale for converting Beaufort Force into wind speed and sample plotting symbols, but these sometimes clutter the map. It is better to make a separate reminder card for the purpose, including perhaps a geostrophic scale along one edge.

Pads of blank charts, of various design, are published by weather offices and by commercial publishers. Alternatively, make up your own blank chart and get it copied in bulk, or place two or three underneath perspex and use with a chinagraph pencil. It can be important to have a sequence in tricky situations, so never be too quick to destroy the last chart when you have made the next.

When taking down the bulletin from dictation, the important thing is to keep a calm and un-thinking state of mind. Get prepared for the bulletin a few minutes before it is due, look at the last chart to refresh your memory about the systems likely to be featured, and then start writing *without* thinking about what it means. The reader may be strictly rationed to a few minutes on the air. The more variable the weather, the longer the message is likely to be and the faster he will have to dictate. If you start thinking to yourself '. . . that's a gale warning for my area, I had better put into harbour instead of proceeding to . . .' you have lost the next piece of information. In trying to recall what it was, you lose the next so that the final result may not be worth having. Just write down like an automaton in the left hand section and keep the thinking for afterwards. Do not try to put information direct on to the map, because searching for the right place takes time. The best place to practice making charts is in your own home when you can afford to laugh at your first results. Once at sea you must be proficient enough to produce an adequate chart.

There are four categories of time in the Shipping Bulletin.
1 Gale warnings which are in operation *at that moment*.
2 The general synopsis giving the position of pressure centres and fronts at a time *5 or 6 hours previously*. In spite of being out of date it is the latest complete picture for the North Atlantic and western Europe because information takes time to collect from the many sources involved, time to plot and time to analyse and project into the future.
3 On the basis of the general synopsis, sea area forecasts of wind and significant weather are given for *24 hours ahead*. These are couched in general terms, for instance 'SW 4-6, perhaps locally 7, becoming W 6 later', and you must gauge from your position in the sea area when 'later' is likely to be.
4 Finally, weather observations made *1 or 2 hours* previously at a dozen coastal stations, giving wind, significant weather and visibility, pressure and tendency. The weather map you draw will refer to that time.

Gale warnings are dictated in a fixed order, which should be the same as on your chart. Simply run a line down the left hand side of the names, only lifting pen off paper when an area is not mentioned.

The general synopsis is the most difficult part to take down because it sometimes contains names of places for which you have not thought up abbreviations. A few letters clearly written should be enough to jog your memory after the broadcast — Ply for Plymouth, or Swd for Sweden. Be particularly careful about names which can appear the same when scribbled, for instance Iceland and Ireland. Make a habit of using something like IC and IR which you have time to write clearly. Abbreviations for the technical terms soon become instinctive — L for low pressure centre, H for high; WF for warm front, CF for cold front and O for occlusion. An arrow or horizontal straight line for 'moving', so that 'a depression moving north east' becomes 'L-NE'. So long as you understand your own shorthand, that is all that matters.

Sea area forecasts follow the general synopsis and the problem here is directly related to the complexity of the weather situation. If there is a depression moving across any area there are likely to be many wind changes and different forecasts for adjacent sea areas. The reader must dictate fast, and the yachtsman must write quickly. If necessary, to keep pace, leave out visibility unless it is poor or fog, leave out the capping to the triangular shower symbol denoting type of precipitation. Concentrate mainly on getting all the wind changes.

In more settled weather conditions, several adjacent sea areas are likely to have the same forecast. Draw a line down the right hand side of the areas listed together (don't bother with horizontal lines to make a bracket — that takes time!) and write the forecast on a line in the middle of the group. Abbreviate 'perhaps locally' as a comma; use a vertical line for 'becoming'; v for 'variable' and a large C for 'cyclonic'.

Thus North '6-8, perhaps 9 locally, becoming north west 4-6 later' becomes simply 'N 6-8, 9 | NW 4-6'.

Use the international symbols for the weather because they cannot be bettered.

Coastal reports are quite easy to take down, always the same factual message, no additions, just occasionally a report missed altogether. Practice wind notations, like NNE or NE'N, so that you don't stumble over then and be confident about pressure tendency symbols — *rising* is a line upwards and towards the right, *falling* is down towards the right, with a particularly steep slope if pressure is changing quickly. *Steady* is indicated by a horizontal line. If you are pressed for time, leave out all the good visibilities and omit the 9 or 10 prefix to pressure values. It is quite clear that 91, for instance, must refer to 991 mb and that something like 26 must mean 1026 mb.

Plot the data on the map after the whole Shipping Bulletin has been written down.

1. Plot wind, weather and pressures given for coastal stations, in their respective positions. The wind vane is a line from whence the wind is blowing, towards the station circle. Half a feather for each Beaufort Force, always drawn on the clockwise side of the vane.

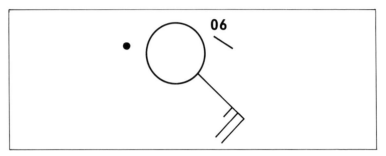

Write pressure on the upper, right, outside of the circle, with tendency below. Significant weather goes centrally outside the left of the circle.

2. Plot centrally into the sea areas (unless there is a contrary instruction) the wind forecast for the next 24 hours. Use black or blue for wind at the beginning of the forecast period, and add a shorter vane in red for changes expected. The two colours help to highlight the differences. If wind is expected to be cyclonic, as the depression passes by, use a large C and enter the Beaufort speed expected.

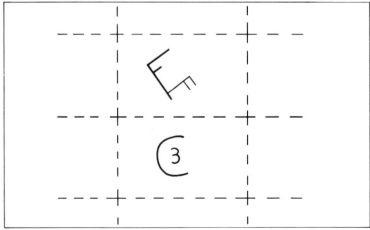

3. Plot centres of high and low pressure, as well as fronts, given in the synopsis and advanced according to speeds suggested or

according to the latest evidence of the plotted coastal reports. If the fronts are not clearly evident, either because of cessation of rain or little wind change, don't worry. It probably means the fronts are dying out and the weather too will be indeterminate.

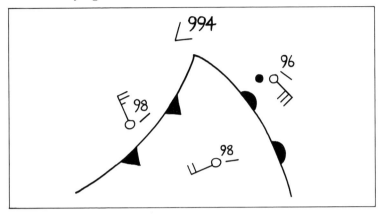

4. Draw the isobars on the map, starting with two equal even values. Join them lightly in pencil, veered slightly from the surface wind. Draw portions of isobars through other even values, and interpolated between odd values. Space according to wind strengths and the geostrophic scale, remembering the isobars will be closer together when wind is stronger.

If you wish to complete the isobar picture over all the sea areas, then you can do so by working backward from the forecast winds given. Place the geostrophic scale over each wind vane and space off a few isobars according to wind strength given. However, the wind pattern is usually quite clear enough without isobars, so one need not bother to do again all the original hard work done by the Met Office. After all, it is wind, not isobars, which concerns a yachtsman at sea!

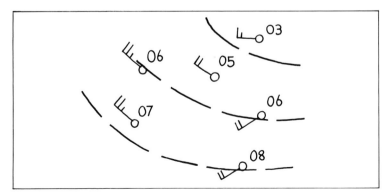

GENERAL SYNOPSIS AT . 0600 .HRS Nov 28

L NW Vik 970 → N

L SWEA → NE to Humber by 0600   990

GALES	SEA AREA FORECAST	WIND, WEATHER, VISIBILITY	
	VIKING		
	N UTSIRE		
	S UTSIRE	W 6-8,9	▽
	FORTIES		
	CROMARTY		
	FORTH		
	TYNE		
	DOGGER		
	FISHER	W 6-8 4	⊖
	GERMAN BT		
	HUMBER		
	THAMES	W 6-8	▽
	DOVER		
	WIGHT	SW 5-7 W	• ▽
	PORTLAND		
	PLYMOUTH	SW-W 5-6 6-8 u5	• ▽
	BISCAY		
	FINISTERRE	W 7-8,9 NW 5-6	• ▽
	SOLE		
	LUNDY	W 3-4 NW 5-6	▽
	FASTNET		
	IRISH SEA	W 5-6	▽
	SHANNON		
	ROCKALL	NW 5-6	▽
	MALIN		
	HEBRIDES	NW 5-7	▽
	MINCHES		
	BAILEY		
	FAIRISLE	NW 6-8	⚡
	FAEROES	NW 5-7,8	⚡ ▽
	SE ICELD	N-NW 6-8	▽

COASTAL REPORTS AT 1200 .HRS

	WIND	WEATHER	VISIBILITY	PRESSURE TENDENCY
TIREE	WNW 1		30	988 ⌐
BUTT LEWIS	NW 4		19	84 ⌐
SUMBURGH	N 2		11	79 —
BELL ROCK	W 4		16	87 —
DOWSING	SW 7		11	994
DOVER	W 4		11	98 ⌐
R.SOVERGN	O		11	98 ⌐
CHANNEL LV	NNE 1	••	4	96 ⌐
SCILLY	NE 3	⸪	3	95 ⌐
VALENTIA	NE 1	•	13	95 ⌐
RONALDSWAY	WSW 5		19	92 ⌐
MALIN HD	WNW 6	·	27	90 ⌐
JERSEY	SE 1		11	95 ⌐

Nautical miles

0   100   200   300   400

Beaufort force   Warm front - knots   Cold front - knots

8 6 5 4   3   2   40 20 10   5   40 20   10   5

If the isobars are not easy to draw, do not be too concerned so long as the wind pattern is self evident from the plotted reports. But if one wind direction from the Coastal Stations is much out of line with the rest, give some thought to the reason. It could be a mistake in transmission; or a local sea breeze variation; or it could portend something worse, as in the plotted chart (opposite).

The General Synopsis indicates a depression somewhere to the south west of England, but all the winds forecast for the southern sea areas are from some westerly point.

This seems to indicate that forecasters are not sure if the

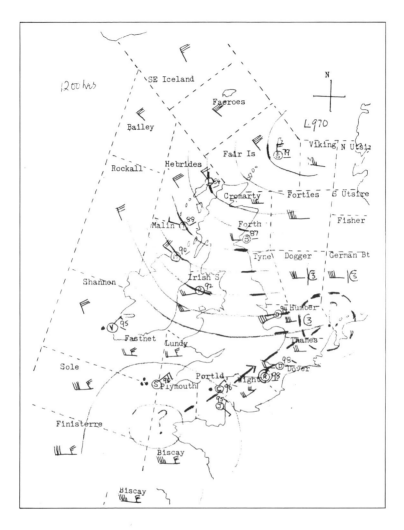

depression will develop to anything much before the end of the forecast period, when they suggest force 3 cyclonic in Humber sea area.

However, look at the light NE wind at Channel Light Vessel, the light SE at Jersey, as well as heavy rain and force 3 NE at Scilly. These seem to indicate a circulation quite close to the English Channel area already, possibly with the centre passing across northern France. This is a warning to listen for every weather report on Local Radio, Coastguard Stations etc, to see how things develop.

Specific meanings of words used in weather forecasts issued by the Meteorological Office (UK).

WIND, BEAUFORT FORCE
Calm 0
Light 1-3
Moderate 4
Fresh 5
Strong 6-7
Gale ....8, gusting to 9
Severe gale ....9, gusting to 10
Storm ....10, gusting to 11

Gale   imminent.................within 6 hours of issue of warning
          soon........................6-12 hours from issue of warning
          later ....more than 12 hours after warning

VISIBILITY
Good ....over 5 nautical miles
Moderate ....2-5 nautical miles
Poor ....1100 yards-2 nautical miles
Fog ....less than 1100 yards
Inland, where there are many points of reference by which to judge visibility, the worst category is subdivided into:
Mist ....200-1100 yards
Fog ....less than 200 yards
Dense fog ....less than 50 yards

PRESSURE TENDENCY, CHANGE IN LAST THREE HOURS
Steady ....less than 0·1 mb
Falling (or rising) slowly ....0·1-1·5 mb
Falling (or rising) ....1·6-3·5 mb
Falling (or rising) quickly ....3·6-6·0 mb
Falling (or rising) very rapidly ....more than 6·0 mb

For information about sources of weather reports, radio wave lengths, French weather stations, schedule of Bulletins, sea areas in other European waters, international weather vocabulary etc, see RYA Publication G5, from RYA, Victoria Way, Woking, Surrey GU21 1EQ, published each year.

Charts

of

weather symptoms

The reminder charts overleaf, a double page for each hemisphere, summarize the information given in the rest of this book.

They relate typical skies and synoptic charts with pressure and weather sequences which may be expected to follow.

It is hoped the charts serve as a visual index to weather, just as the verbal index helps locate topics in the text of the book.

Northern hemisphere: typical weather changes consequent upon various cloud symptoms and pressure patterns.		
The sky	Cirrus increasing, cumulus tops flattening	Rainbearing altostratus and stratus covering mountain tops
General situation	Active depression moving E ●●━ Warm front and ▲▲ cold front advancing with speeds measurable by geostrophic scale	Filling depression. Original fronts occluded ▲●▲● and trailing (slack wind parallel to front gives little forward movement). **Beware sudden formation of secondary depression, often more violent than original**
Pressure pattern N ↑ W ———— E ↓ S		
Pressure	＼ Falls till warm front arrives — Steadies in warm sector ／ Rises sharply behind cold front	∧ Falls sharply after brief rise behind occlusion Then as in Column 1
Cloud	⌐ Cirrus increases to obscure sun, then ⫽ thickens to flat, grey altostratus with low --- stratus in rain belt ◠ Small cumulus in warm sector in summer - - - Stratus in warm sector in winter ⌂ Cumulonimbus along cold front, clearing dramatically behind front	⌐ As in Column 1 ⫽ --- ◠ - - - ⌂
Wind N ↑ W ———— E ↓ S	South of centre ↺ backing till warm front arrives ↻ veering behind warm front ↻ veering again behind cold front North of centre ↺ backing all the time **Attention for gale warnings if pressure falling fast**	Changing according to position relative to new centre **Attention for gale warnings**
Weather	• Cloudy, leading to rain , Cloudy with drizzle in warm sector in winter ▽⩍ Thundery showers and squalls at cold front, becoming fair behind cold front	• As in Column 1 , ▽⩍

Cumulonimbus	Fair weather cumulus	Fog
Old depression, centre almost stationary, original fronts dissipated. **Beware sudden formation of troughs even if not indicated on previous charts**	Ridge of high pressure behind cold front, often only a temporary sandwich between one low pressure system and next	Anticyclone or high pressure area. Little pressure gradient over whole chart
⟍ Slight fall ahead of troughs ⟋ Slight rise behind troughs	⟋ Rises sharply behind cold front ⟍ Steadies and falls if another depression advancing	— Slow, steady rise
⌒ Cumulonimbus, in unbroken line along troughs	⌒ Large cumulus at first ⌒ Decreasing to small cumulus ⌇ Cirrus increasing if another front advancing	Cumulus gradually dispersing, becoming cloudless Occasional thin stratus at night, dispersing in morning according to season. Sometimes persists on coast even in summer
Gusty with extreme changes in wind direction near cumulonimbus	↺ Backing if another front approaching	Light and variable. Sea breezes develop on summer days
▽▽ Frequent thundery showers, prolonged in trough lines, with squalls	▽ Occasional showers at first dying out, becoming fair	Fine but hazy in summer ≡ Fog inland in winter

NORTHERN HEMISPHERE

Southern hemisphere: typical weather changes consequent upon various cloud symptoms and pressure patterns.		
The sky	Cirrus increasing, cumulus tops flattening	Rainbearing altostratus and stratus covering mountain tops
General situation	Active depression moving E Warm front and cold front advancing with speeds measurable by geostrophic scale	Filling depression. Original fronts occluded and trailing (slack wind parallel to front gives little forward movement). **Beware sudden formation of secondary depression, often more violent than original**
Pressure pattern N W—E S		
Pressure	Falls till warm front arrives Steadies in warm sector Rises sharply behind cold front	Falls sharply after brief rise behind occlusion Then as in Column 1
Cloud	Cirrus increases to obscure sun, then thickens to flat, grey altostratus with low stratus in rain belt Small cumulus in warm sector in summer Stratus in warm sector in winter Cumulonimbus along cold front, clearing dramatically behind front	As in Column 1
Wind N W—E S	North of centre veering till warm front arrives backing behind warm front backing again behind cold front South of centre veering all the time **Attention for gale warnings if pressure falling fast**	Changing according to relative position of new centre **Attention for gale warnings**
Weather	• Cloudy, leading to rain , Cloudy with drizzle in warm sector in winter Thundery showers and squalls at cold front, becoming fair behind cold front	• As in Column 1

Cumulonimbus	Fair weather cumulus	Fog
Old depression, centre almost stationary, original fronts dissipated. **Beware sudden formation of troughs even if not indicated on previous charts**	Ridge of high pressure behind cold front, often only a temporary sandwich between one low pressure system and next	Anticyclone or high pressure area. Little pressure gradient over whole chart
⌐ Slight fall ahead of troughs / Slight rise behind troughs	/ Rises sharply behind cold front ⌐ Steadies and falls if another depression advancing	/ Slow, steady rise
⌂ Cumulonimbus, in unbroken line along troughs.	⌂ Large cumulus at first ⌒ Decreasing to small cumulus 2 Cirrus increasing if another front advancing	Cumulus gradually dispersing, becoming cloudless Occasional thin stratus at night, dispersing in morning according to season. Sometimes persists on coast even in summer
Gusty with extreme changes in wind direction near cumulonimbus	↻ Veering if another front approaching	Light and variable. Sea breezes develop on summer days
▽∀ Frequent thundery showers, prolonged in trough lines, with squalls	▽ Occasional showers at first, dying out, becoming fair	Fine but hazy in summer ≡ Fog inland in winter

SOUTHERN HEMISPHERE

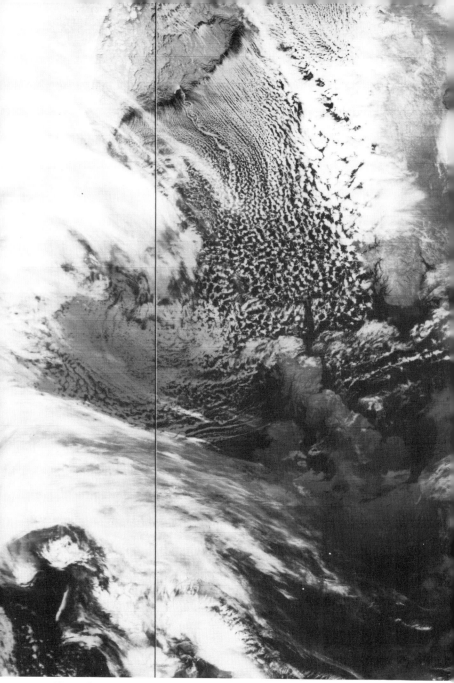

View of north Atlantic on infra-red wave length, 17 February 1978. The land is colder (therefore lighter) than the sea; cumulus clouds form over the sea as soon as cold air blows off the ice cap and get bigger as they move southwards. Two depressions approach from the west, but the British Isles are almost cloud free in a ridge of high pressure. *Courtesy of Dundee University.*

Index

Colour Pictures, between page numbers, in bold.